The Foreign Service Traveler

James Rivera

Author: James Rivera
Publisher: Rivera Investment R.I.C.O LLC
Photograph Locations:
Bangkok, Thailand 2010
Bandar Seri Begawan, Brunei 2010
Addis Ababa, Ethiopia 2010
Luxembourg, the Grand Duchy of Luxembourg 2009
Manama, Bahrain 2009

ISBN-10 0615453430
ISBN-13 9780615453439

About the Photographer:

My name is James Rivera, and I'm a 28 year-old Miami native of Cuban descent. I've been interested in photography ever since I was a child, when my mother would dress me in various strange outfits and subject me to the fascinating snapping of her camera. I was further captivated by the scores of professional photographers seen shooting around Miami, attracted by its pristine beaches.

These experiences inspired me to sign up for a course in graphic design at my High School. Admittedly, I chose it because it was the least-difficult option to fill out my class schedule, but in retrospect, it has turned out to be one of my most influential adolescent experiences, and the driving force that pushed me to study photography.

While never having received any formal training, I devoured books about photography. Once the internet reached its true potential I began to research online for more information on photography. I began experimenting with photography in the era of film cameras, and moved to one of the first digital cameras released by Kodak in the late 90's. I couldn't understand why my older film camera produced better results than my shiny new Kodak, a question which furthered my curiosity regarding the dynamics and technology of photography. While pursuing that answer, I fell back to using the film camera until years later when digital cameras finally started to catch up in terms of image quality. Now I utilize both types, depending upon the situation.

The Unique Views of a U.S. Diplomat:

While I dream of being able to support my family with my photography, my 'day job' definitely doesn't hurt. As a computer and telephone technician for the Department of State, I'm constantly travelling to different U.S. Embassies all over the world. U.S. Foreign Service officers travel not only to the Parises and Londons of the world, but also to parts of the world not normally accessible to tourists. These include poverty-stricken regions, war-torn countries, and even places where tourists normally do not travel. Currently based in Washington D.C., in just two years I've visited Manama, Bahrain; Luxembourg; Addis Ababa, Ethiopia; Bangkok Thailand; Bandar, Brunei; and many other fascinating places. While quite busy during the day, I've taken advantage of my nights and weekends to explore and photograph these exotic locales.

Cameras Fit for a Diplomat:

When I visit a new country, I try to capture the essence of that country. That means shooting not only the scenic areas, but also the not-so-scenic. Sometimes these not-so-scenic places are poverty-stricken and/or have questionable security, making carrying a big, expensive camera impractical. In these places, I've found that my point and shoot Nikon is inconspicuously small enough to carry around in my pocket, while providing outstanding images for a point-and-shoot camera.

If I can manage, however, I generally prefer the images produced by one of my two film cameras: the Nikon N80 and the Nikon F4. That said, some of the latest digital models have achieved such absurdly high resolutions that the argument that film is intrinsically sharper is becoming harder to defend.

The 'Art' of PhotoShopping:

As I mentioned before, my High School graphics design class led me into photography. The class used old Apple computers running PhotoShop 3.0. As a result, I've been using Adobe products like PhotoShop and Lightroom to retouch my photos.

I've often heard the quip that "true photography is taking great shots without the need to do any post-processing." While I don't entirely disagree, I would point out that in our retouched digital world, it may not be possible to shoot an image (with analog equipment alone) as perfect as can be achieved in the digital realm. Modern digital cameras go so far as to do some processing of the image data before it is even saved to a file. What's more, I would argue that the process of digitally manipulating the lighting, detail, and coloration of a photograph is an art in and of itself, and therefore should not be disparaged.

Why I Love Black & White:

For me, photography is both a form of self-expression and a way to project different feelings and emotions onto the viewer. I tend to focus on black and white pictures, as I feel they allow me to dictate what my audience will focus on more precisely than full color shots. With shadowing and lighting, I can significantly alter the mood of a black and white photo and, in turn, its impact on the observer. In my opinion, when people see pictures in color, they often get lost in the nature of the hues and vastness of the image. Black and white allows me to tightly control the focus and tell a story with the image.

Bangkok,Thailand

The following photos were taken in downtown Bangkok, with in a one mile radius of my hotel. I have been there twice, each time for only 24 hours, which means I didn't have much time to explore; even though my stay was short I love that country and its people. The streets are clean, the people are pleasant, the food is great and anything you can think of they have. Due to the exchange rate, gifts, food, travel and site seeing are all inexpensive. If I had to pick a place to retire I would definitely choose Thailand.

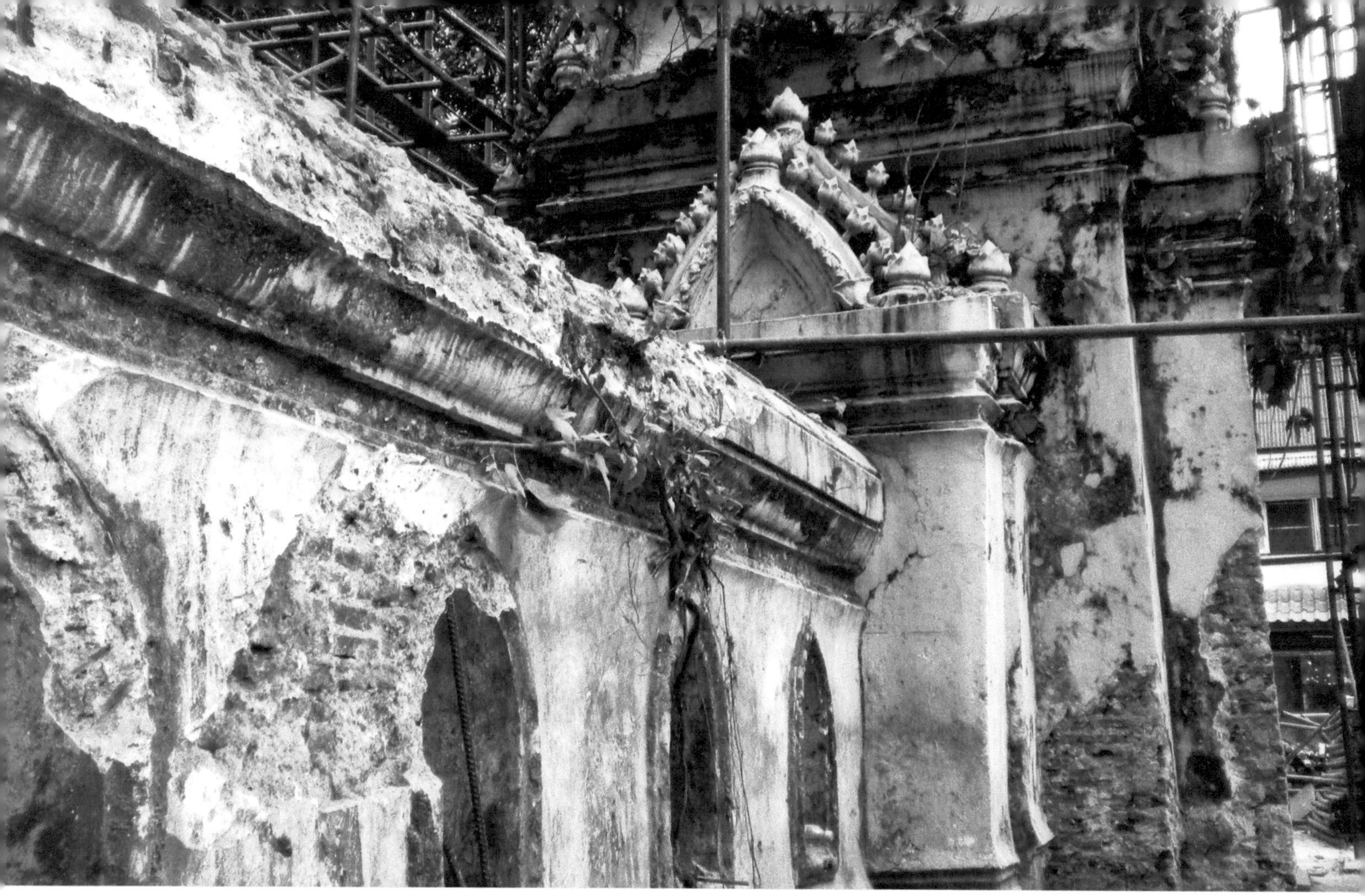

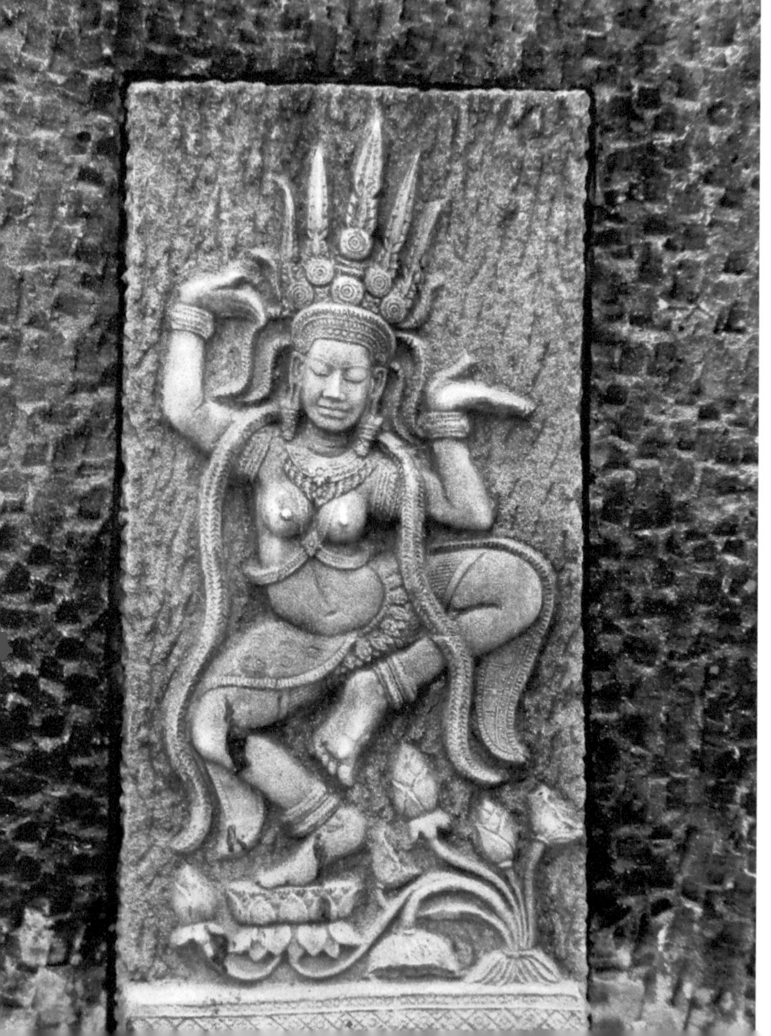

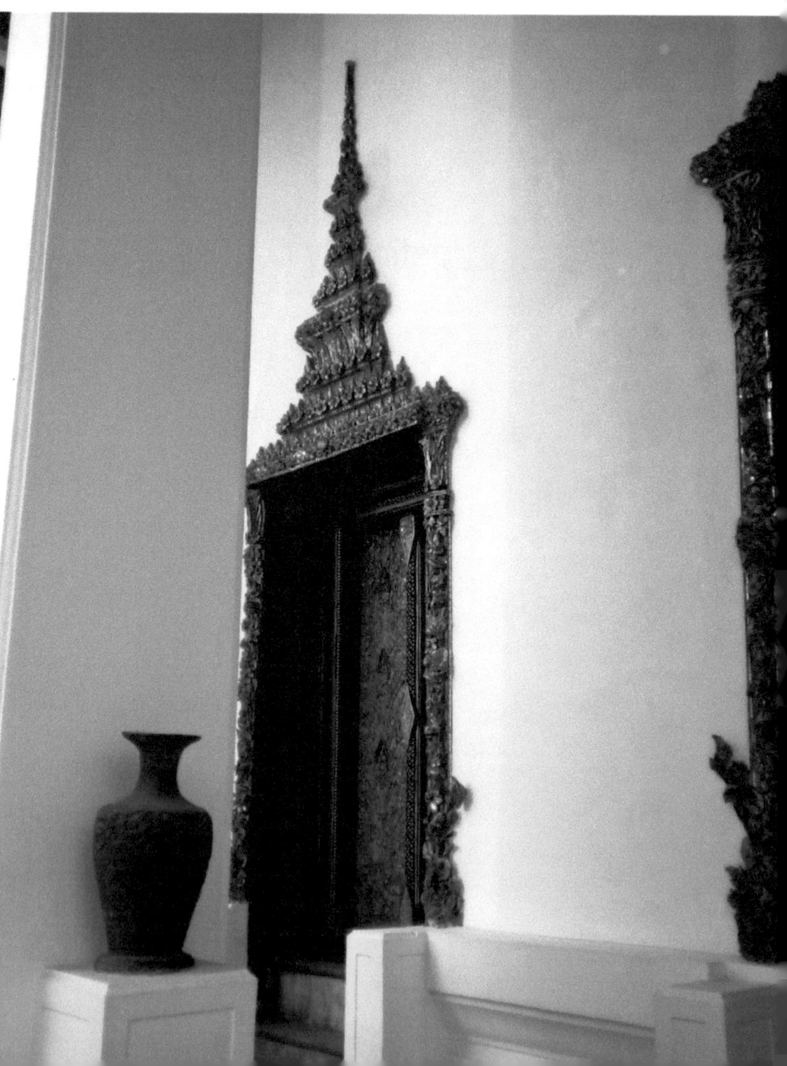

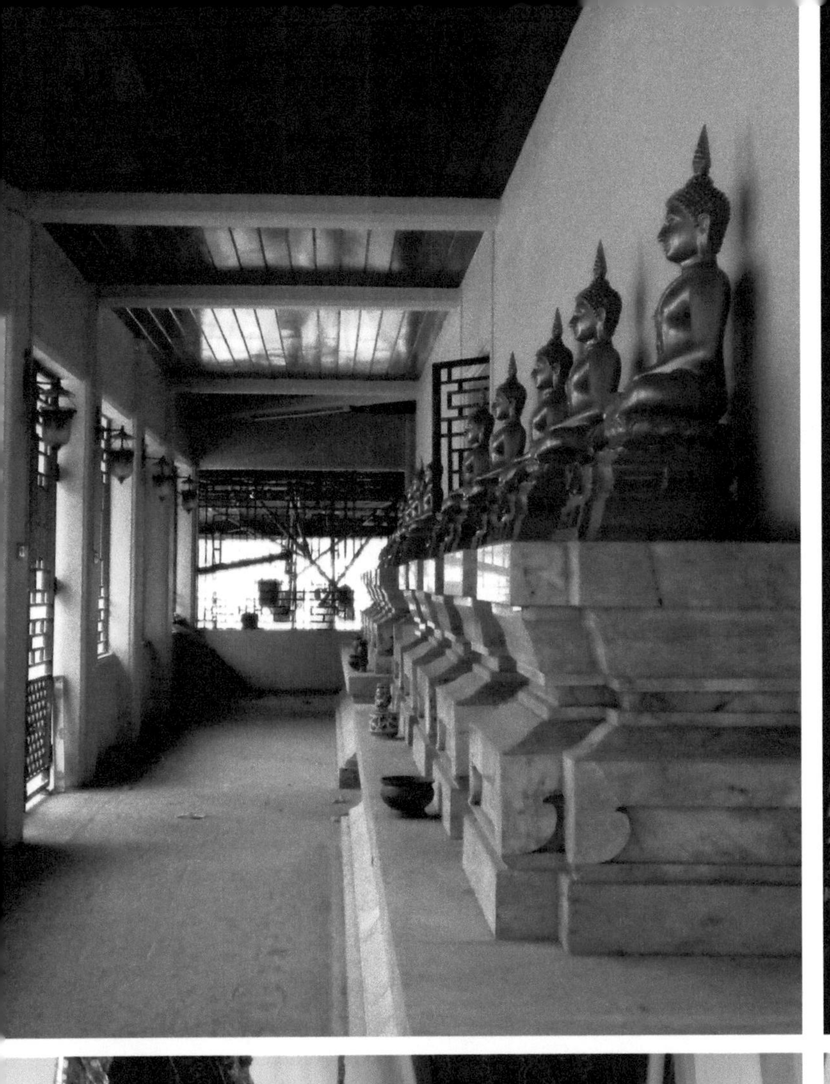
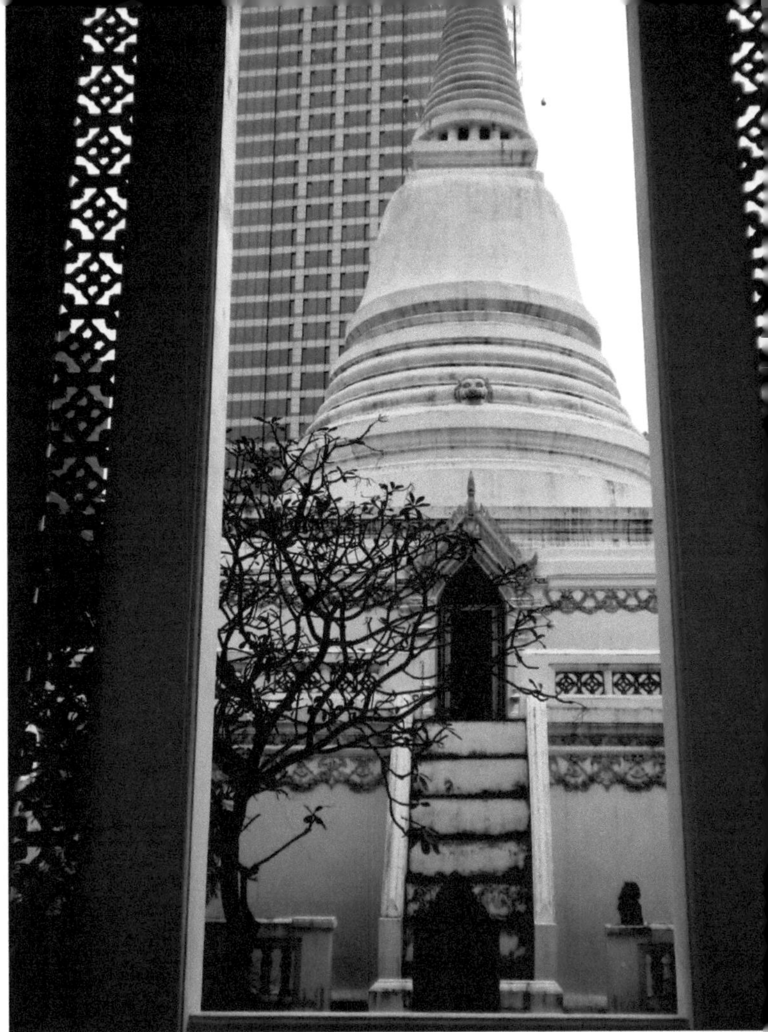
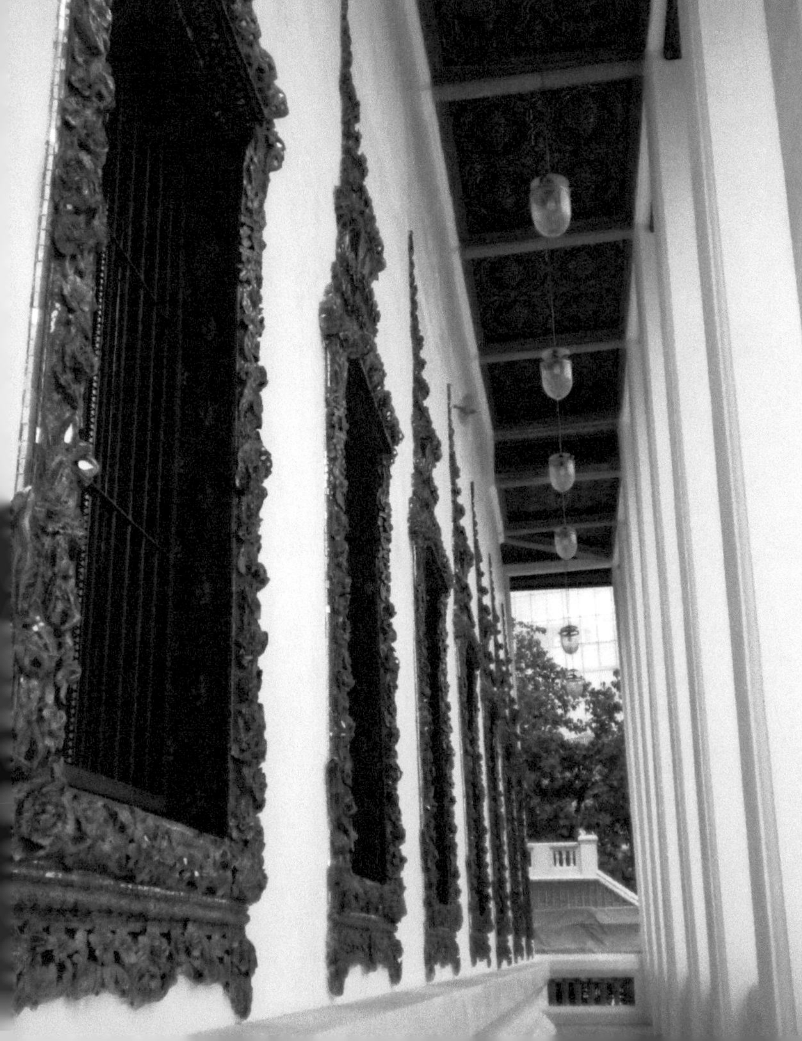
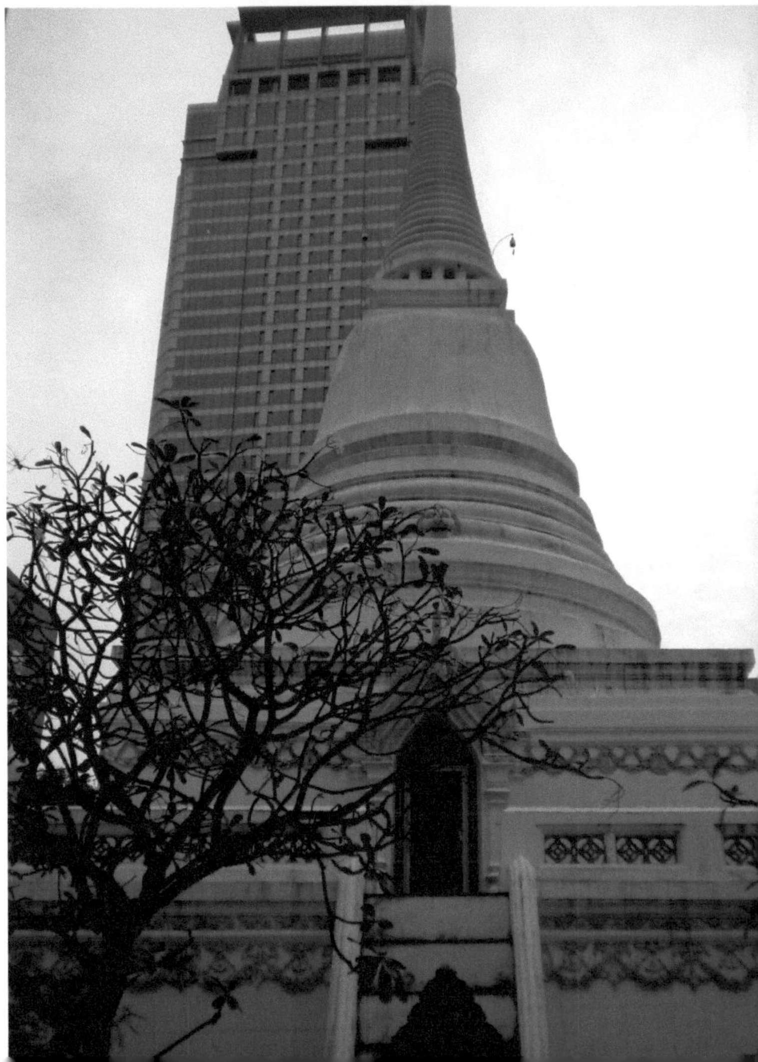

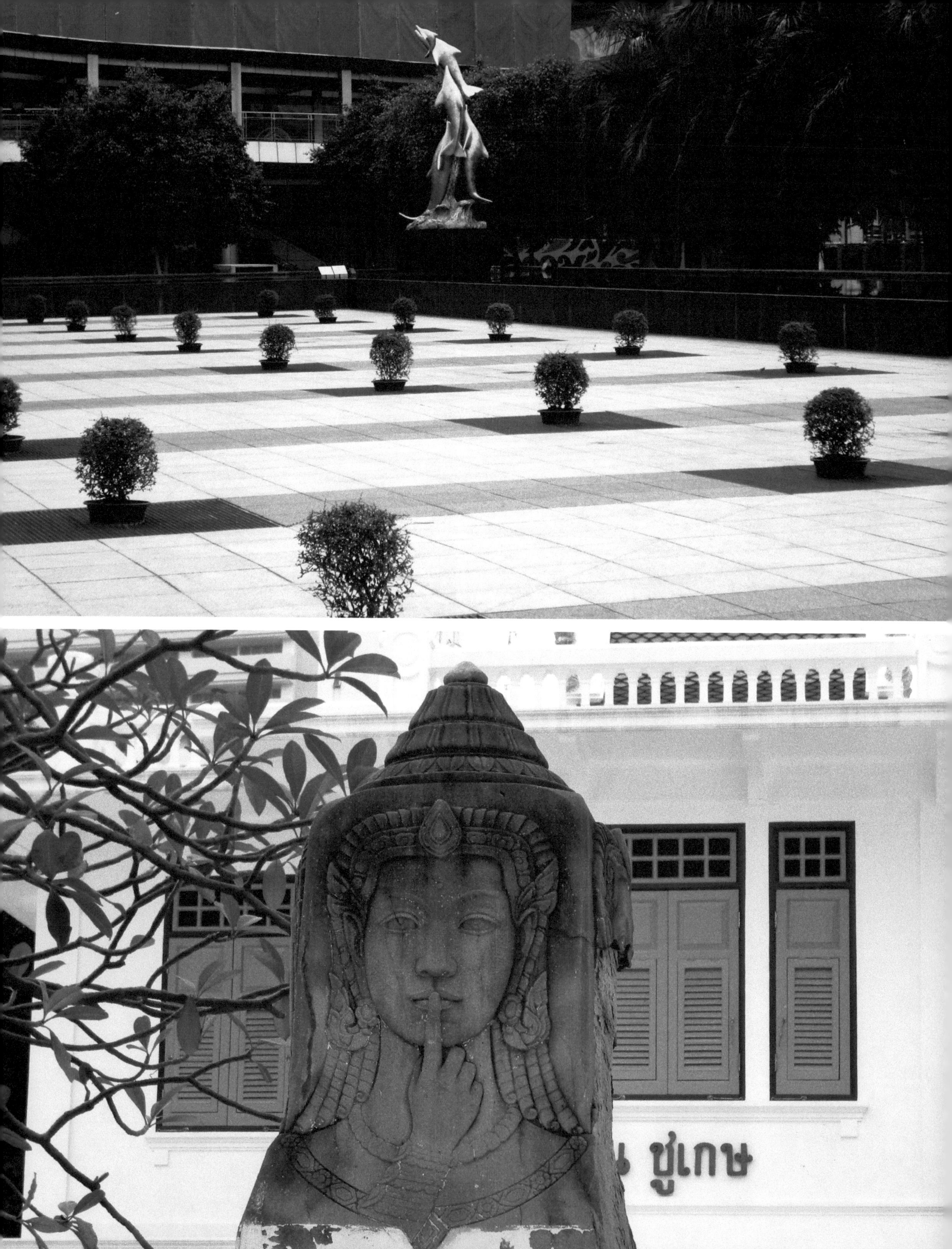
ชูเกษ

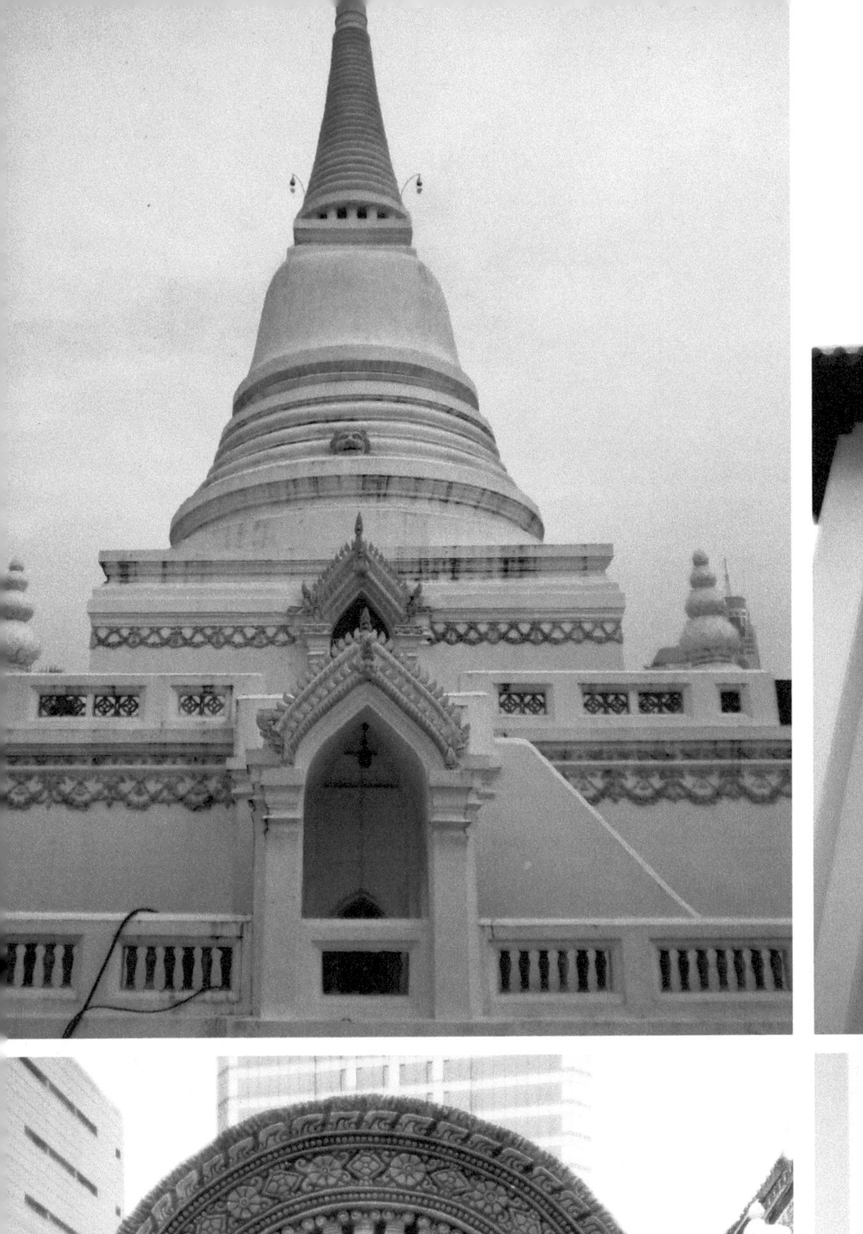
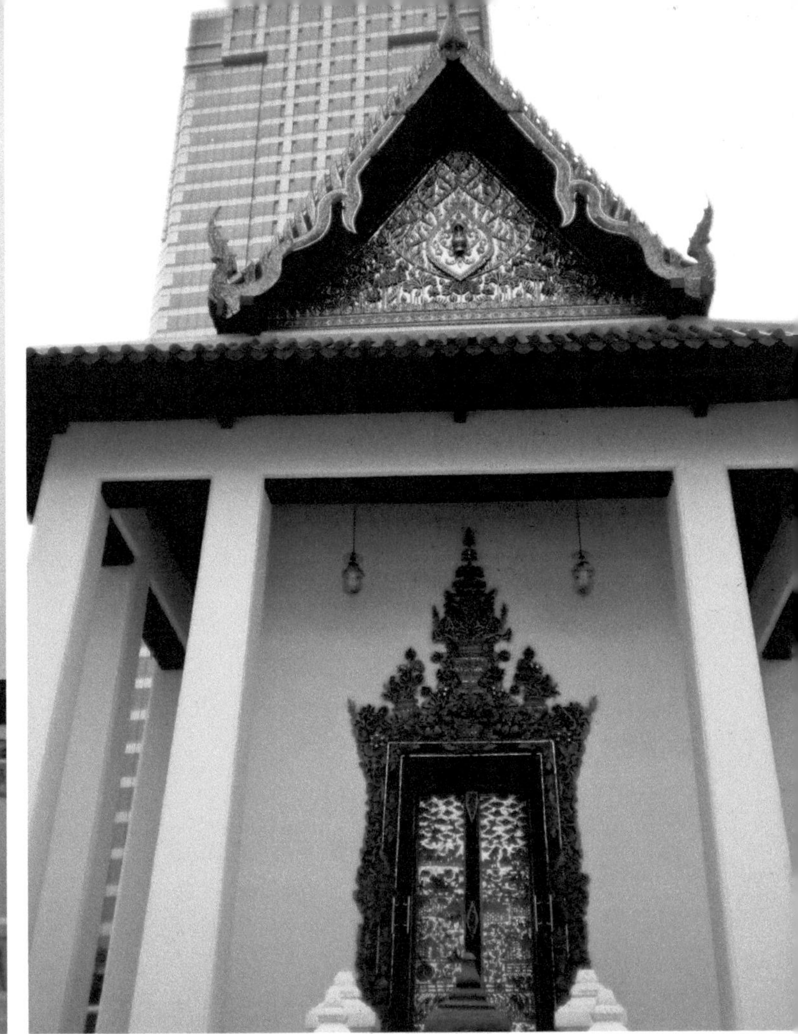
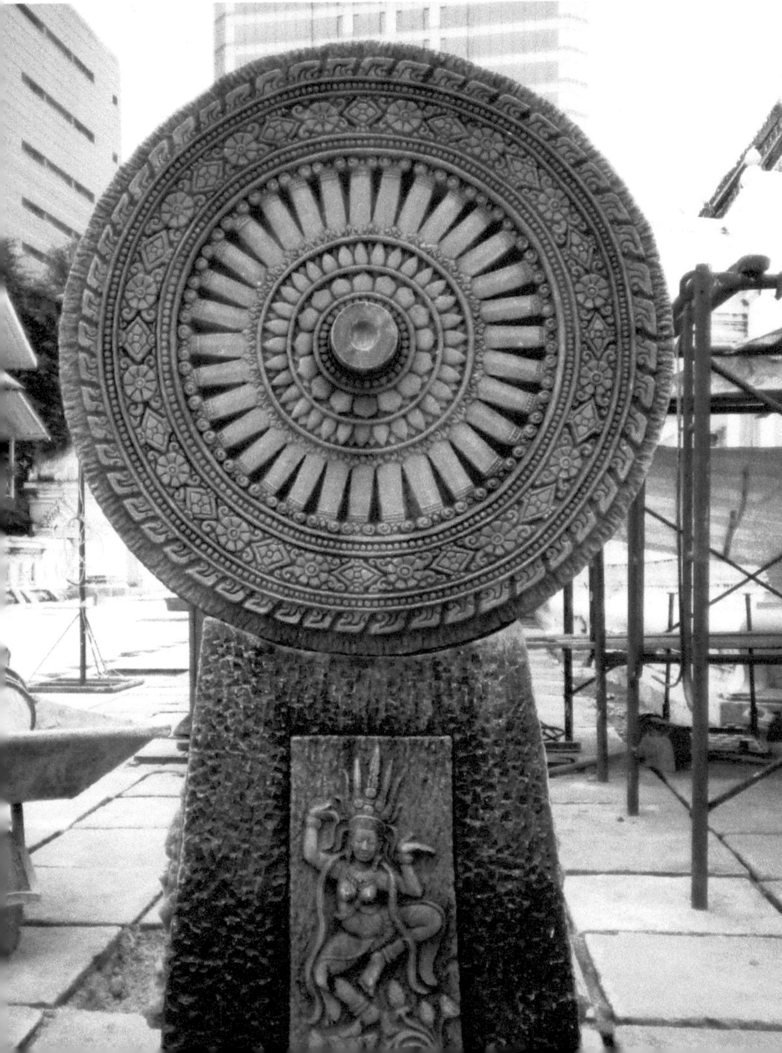
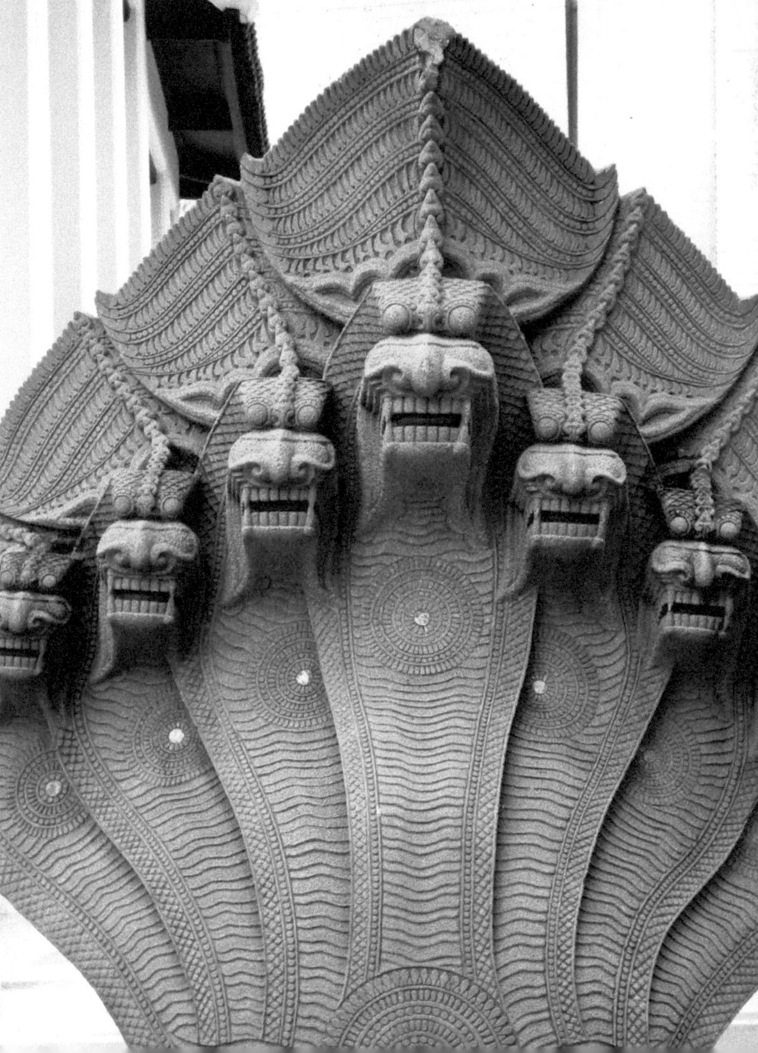

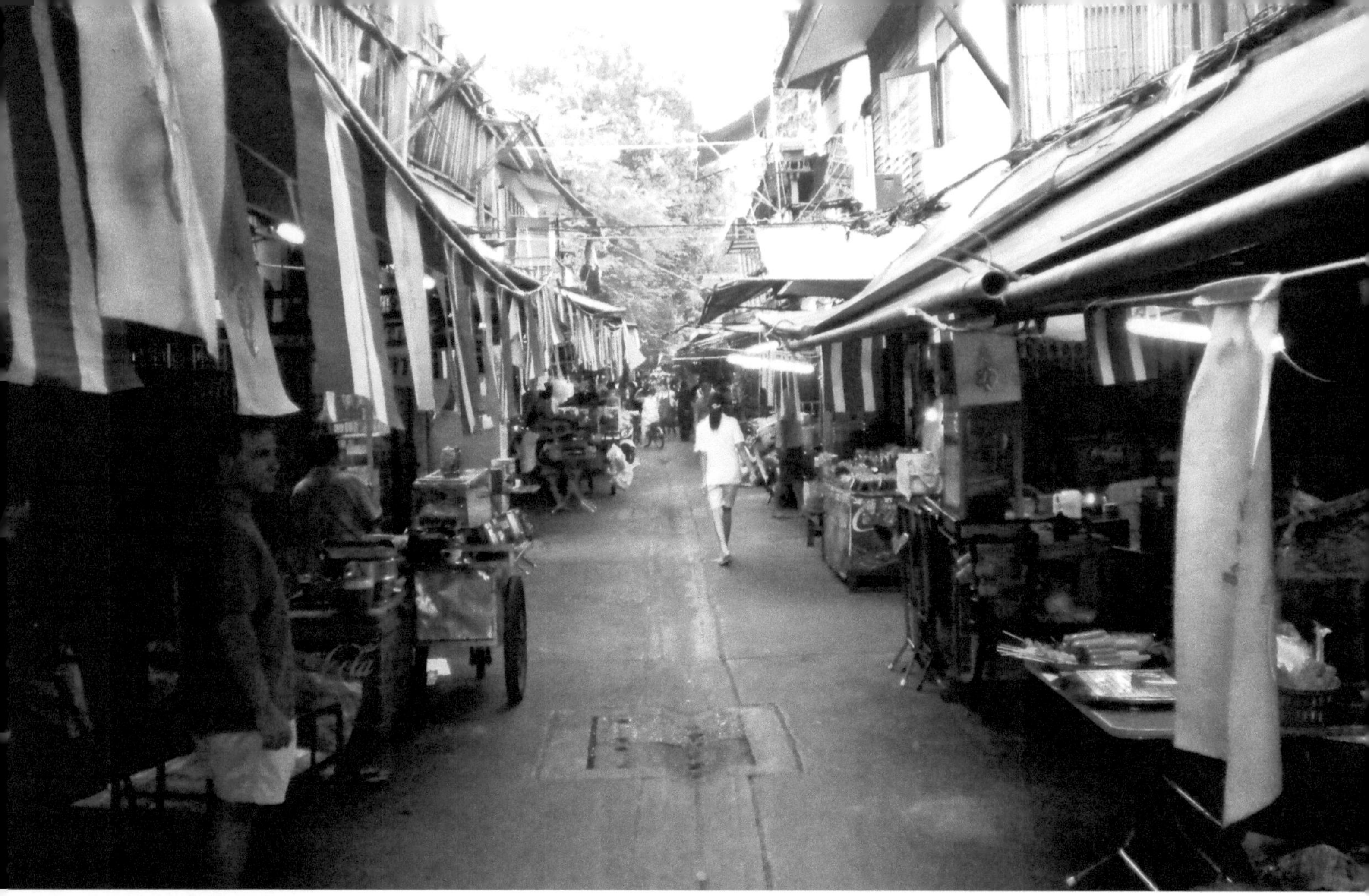

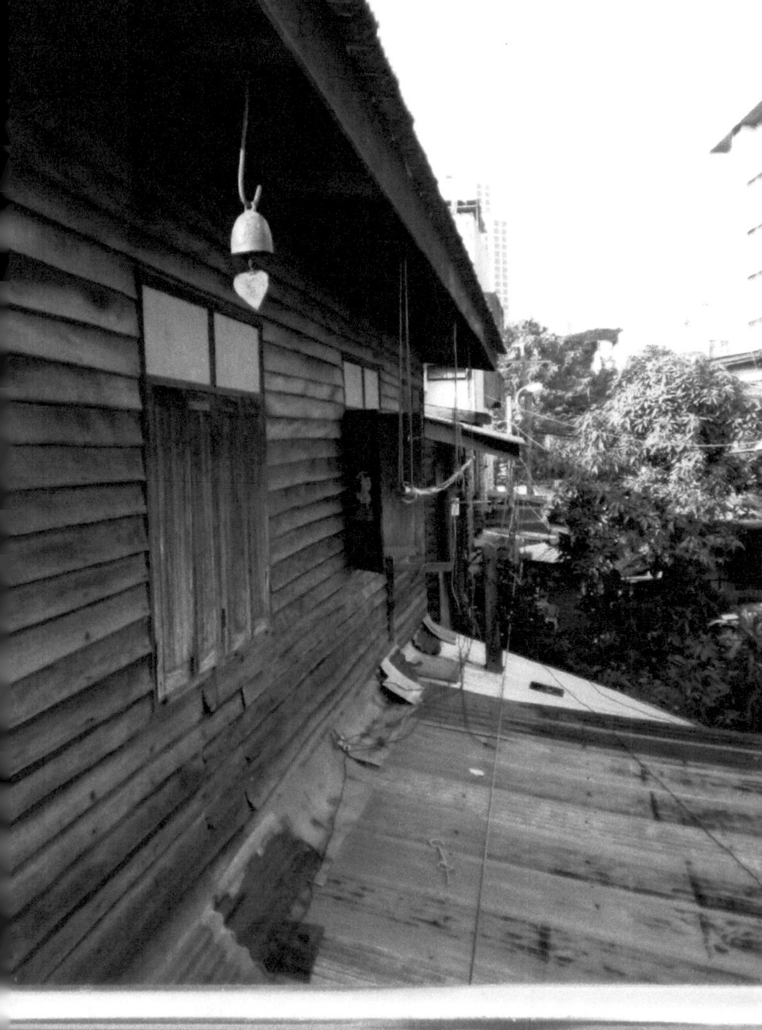

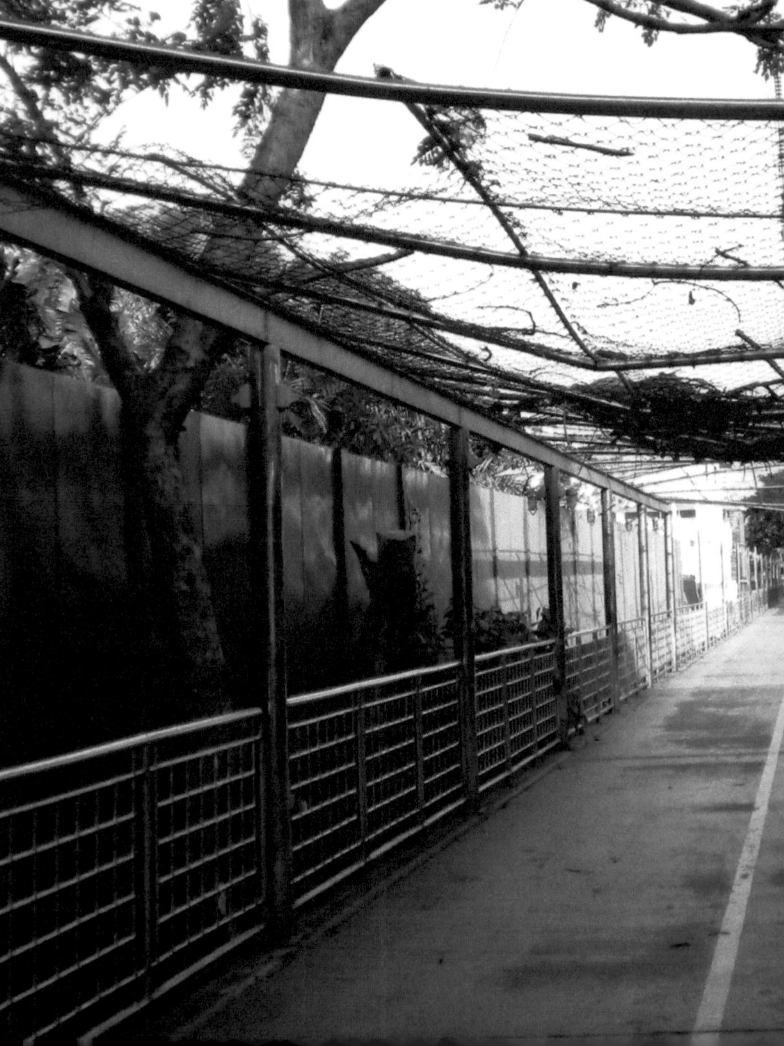

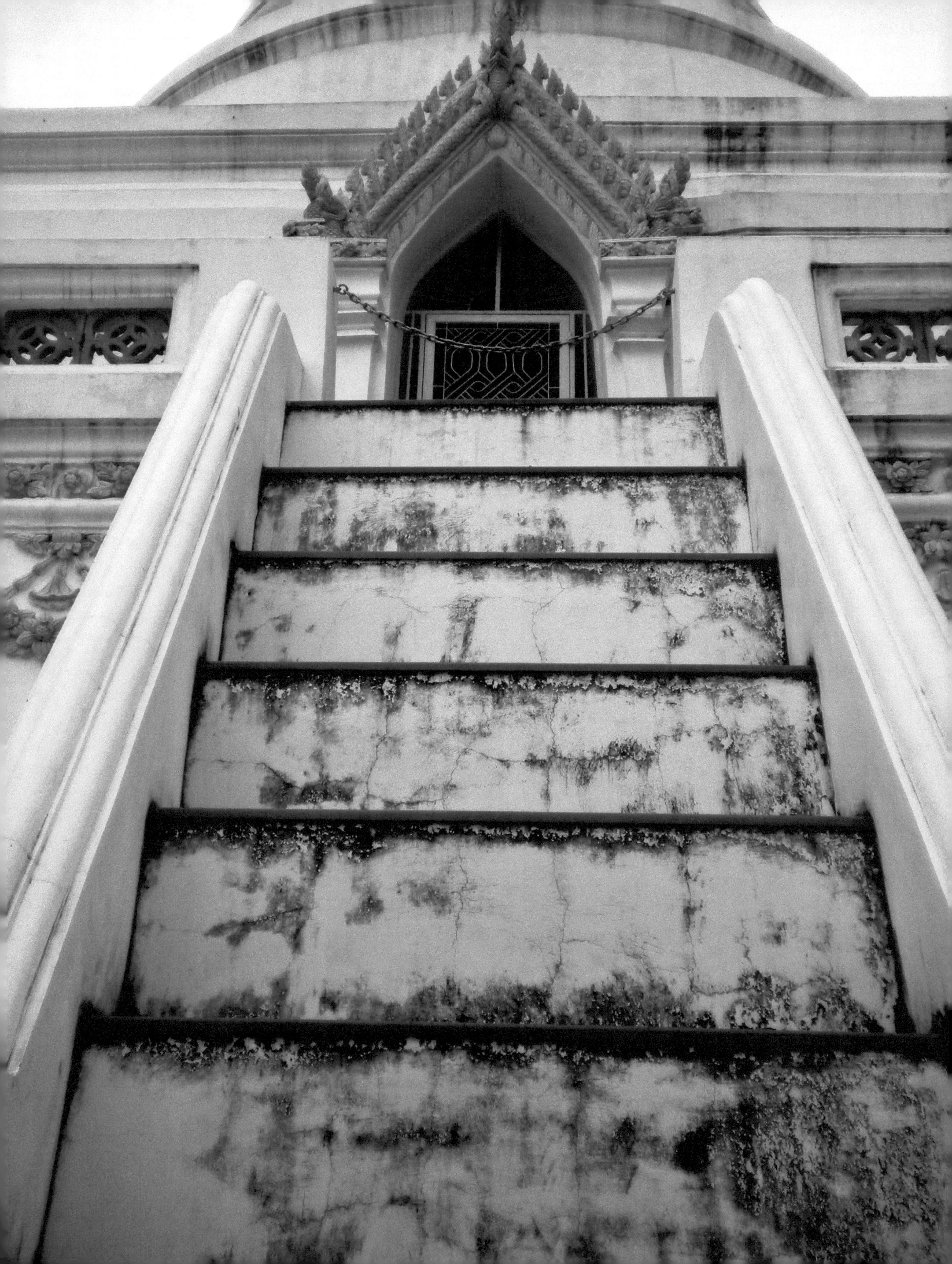

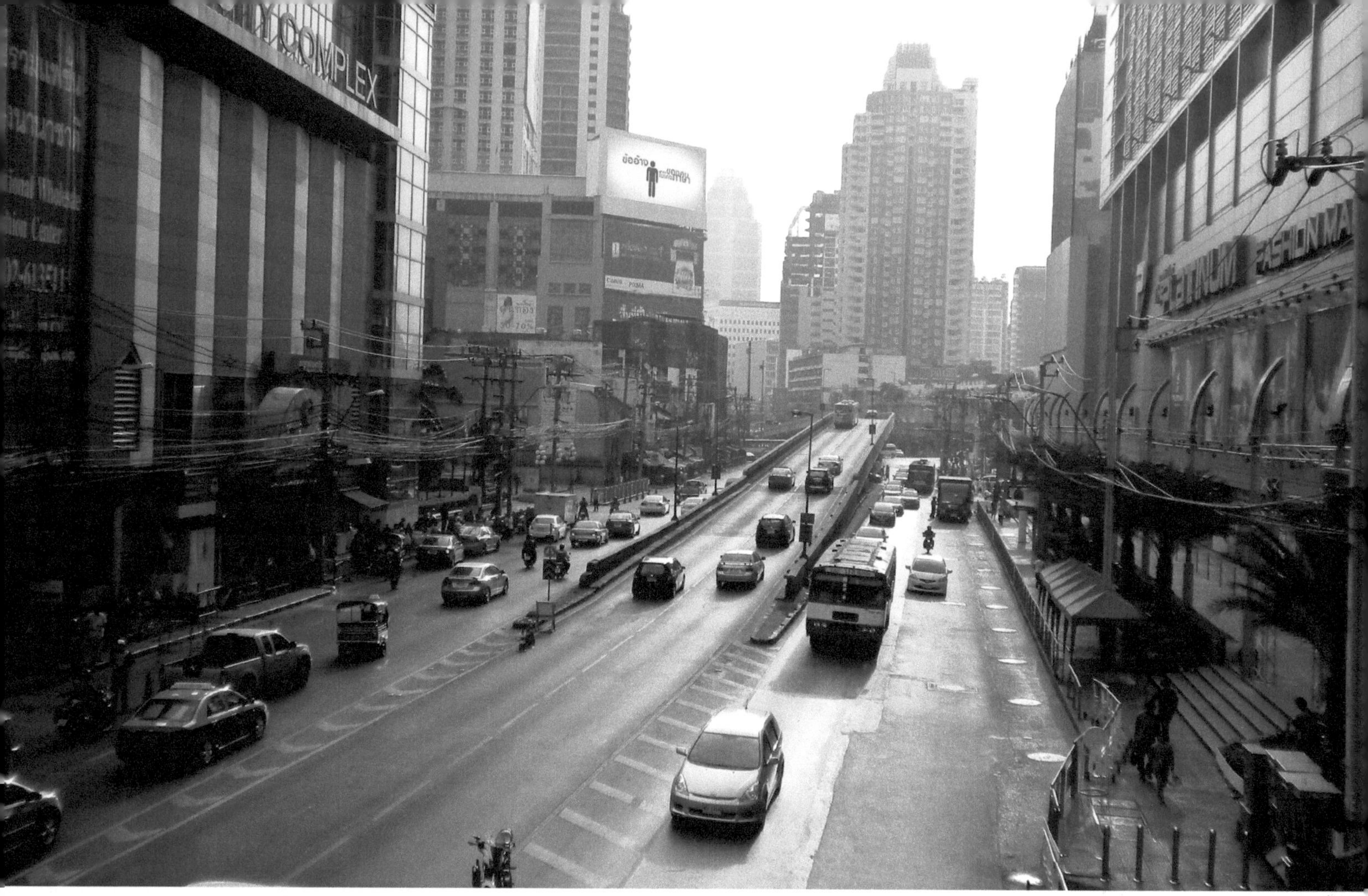

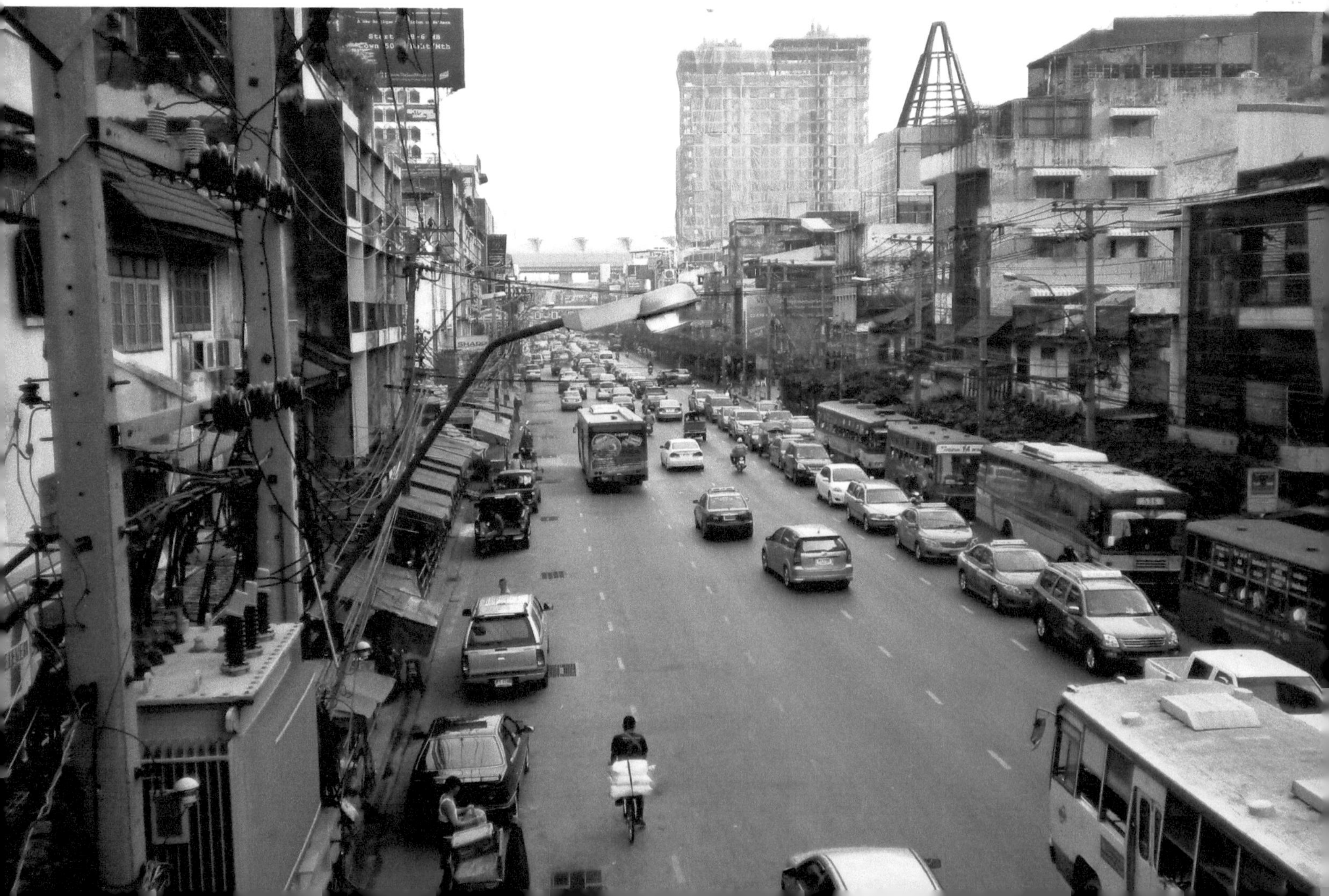

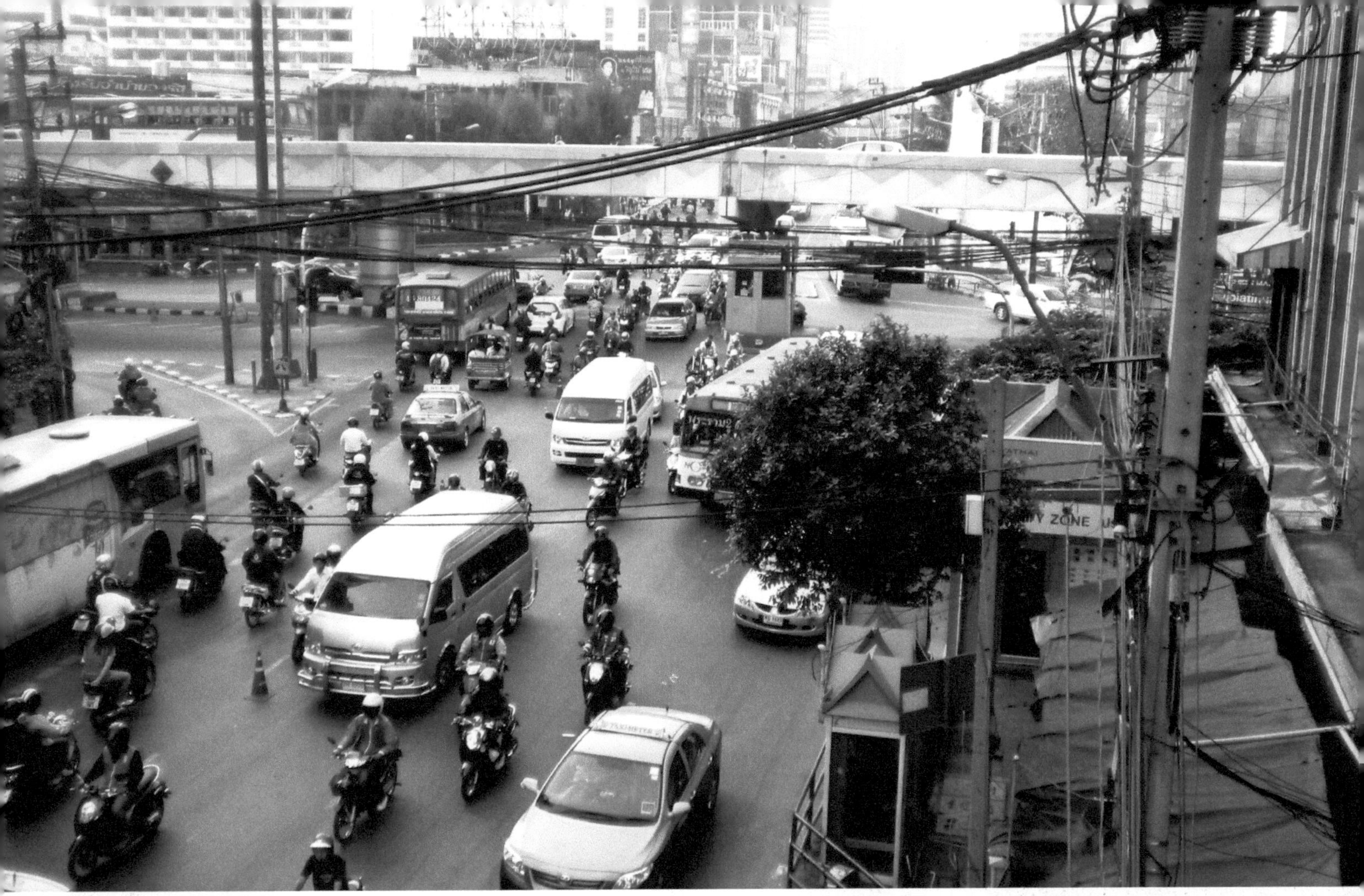

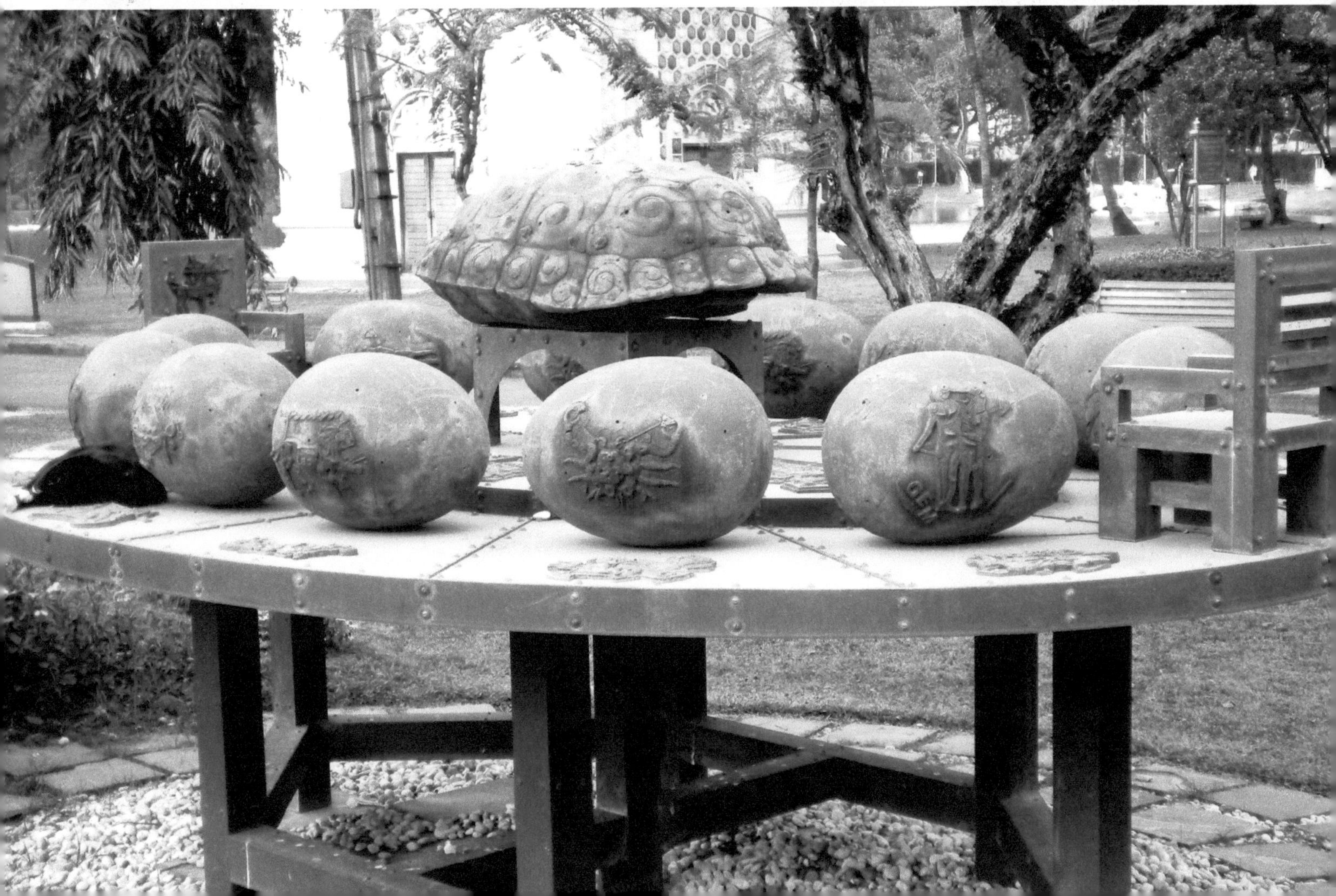

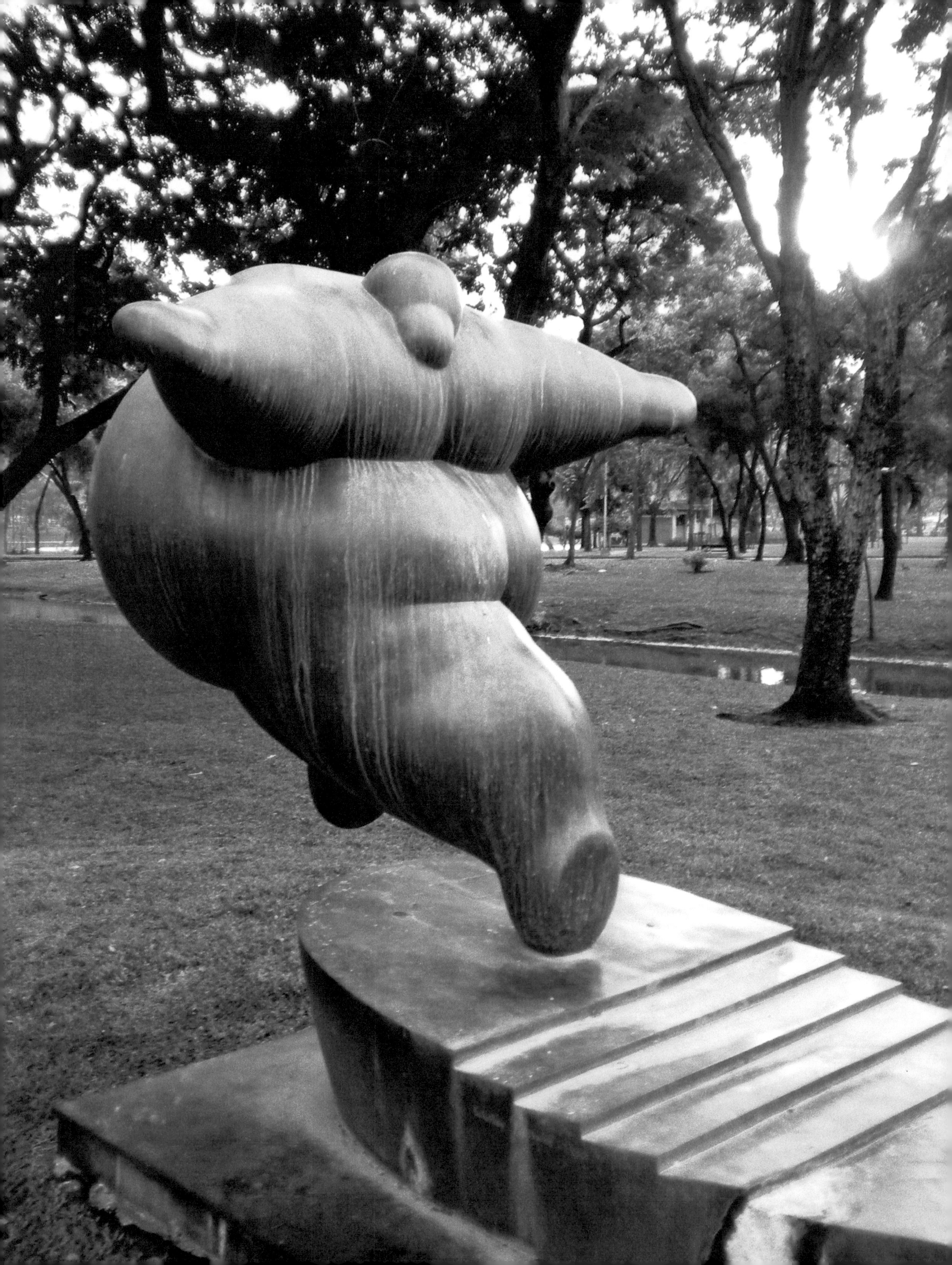

Bandar Seri Begawan, Brunei

The following photos are from Bandar Seri Begawan or BSB for short. Most of these pictures were taken in downtown BSB, where it was easy to walk around and take pictures. I had never heard of this country or known its location. I traveled to BSB to transfer all of the US Embassy communications equipment from the old Embassy building to the new Embassy building. I stayed there for a month and was able to enjoy much of what Brunei has to offer.

While in BSB I did not see any clubs, bars or even performing arts theatres. I was so busy with work I probably did not notice them. The people are constantly smiling, the country is extremely clean and the streets are in excellent condition. I enjoyed my stay; but after a month, I missed my family and was eager to go back home.

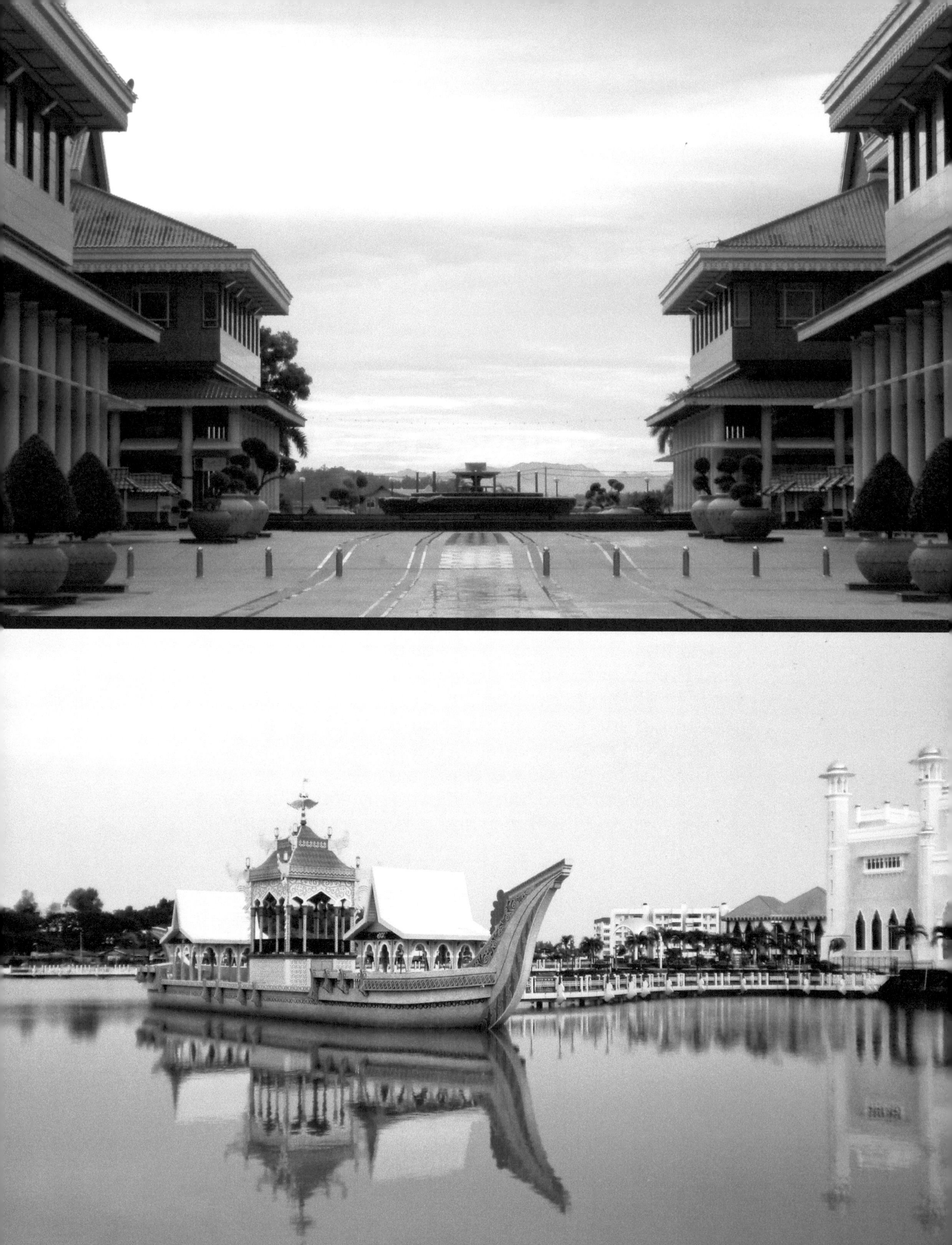

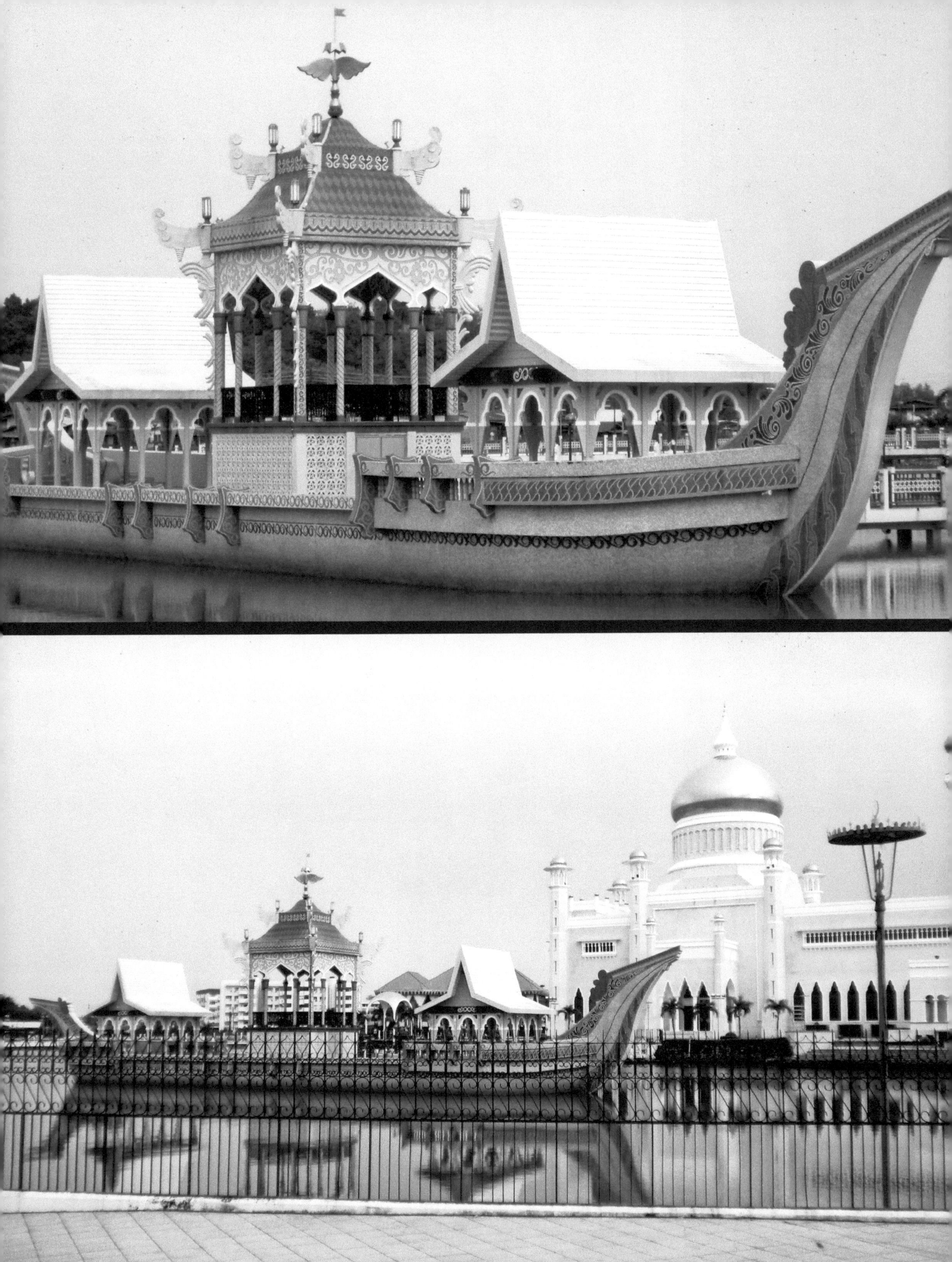

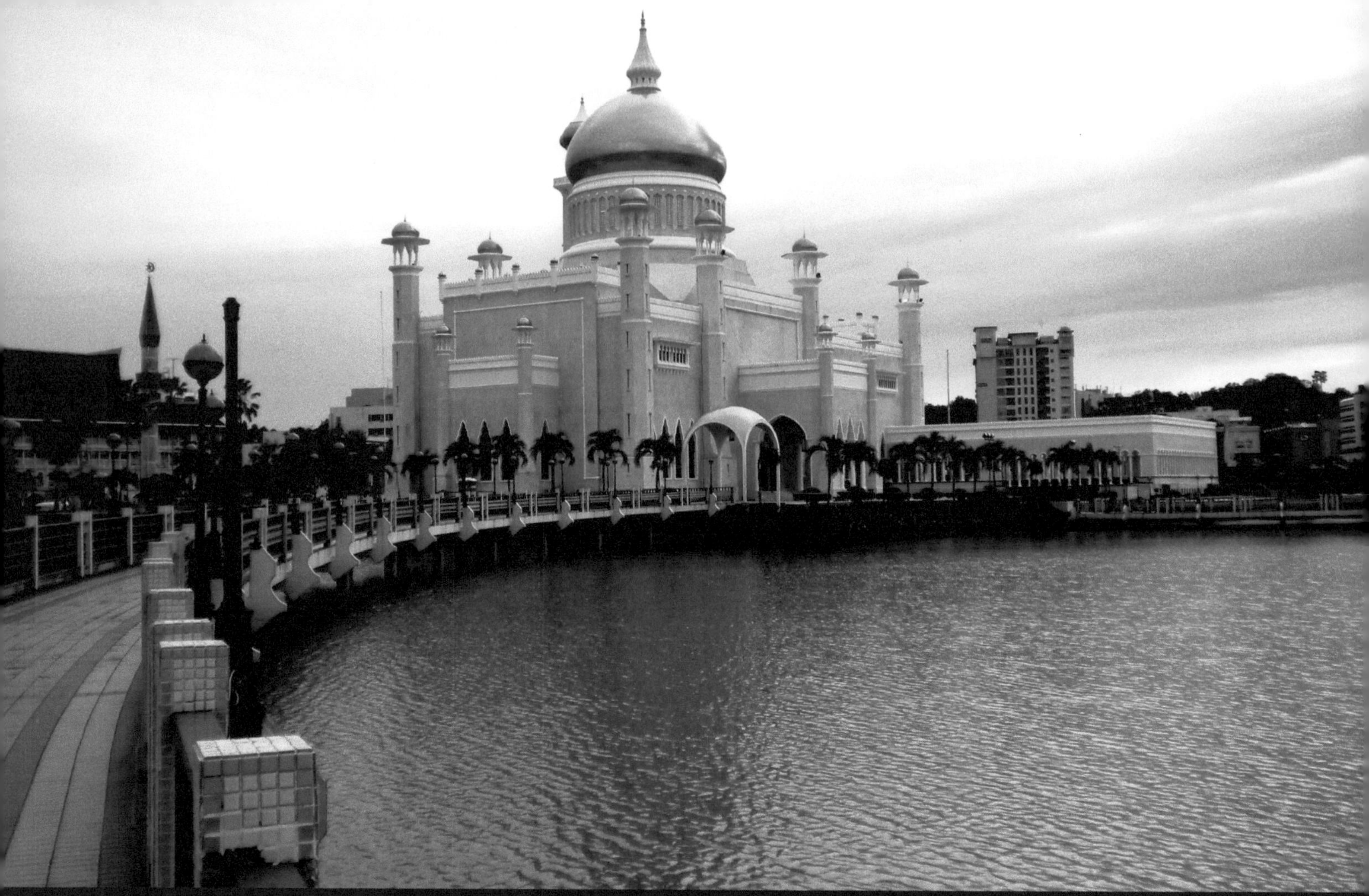

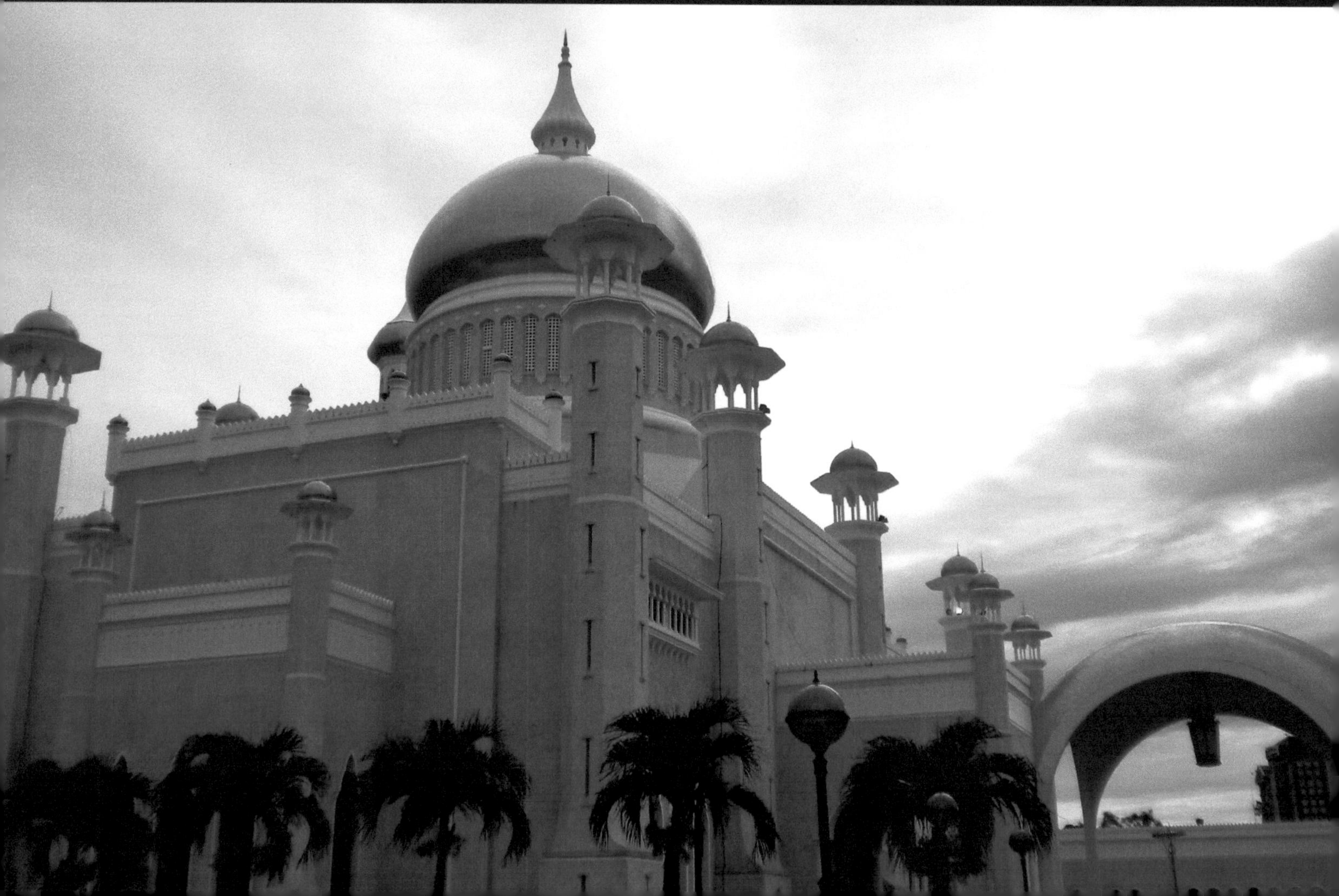

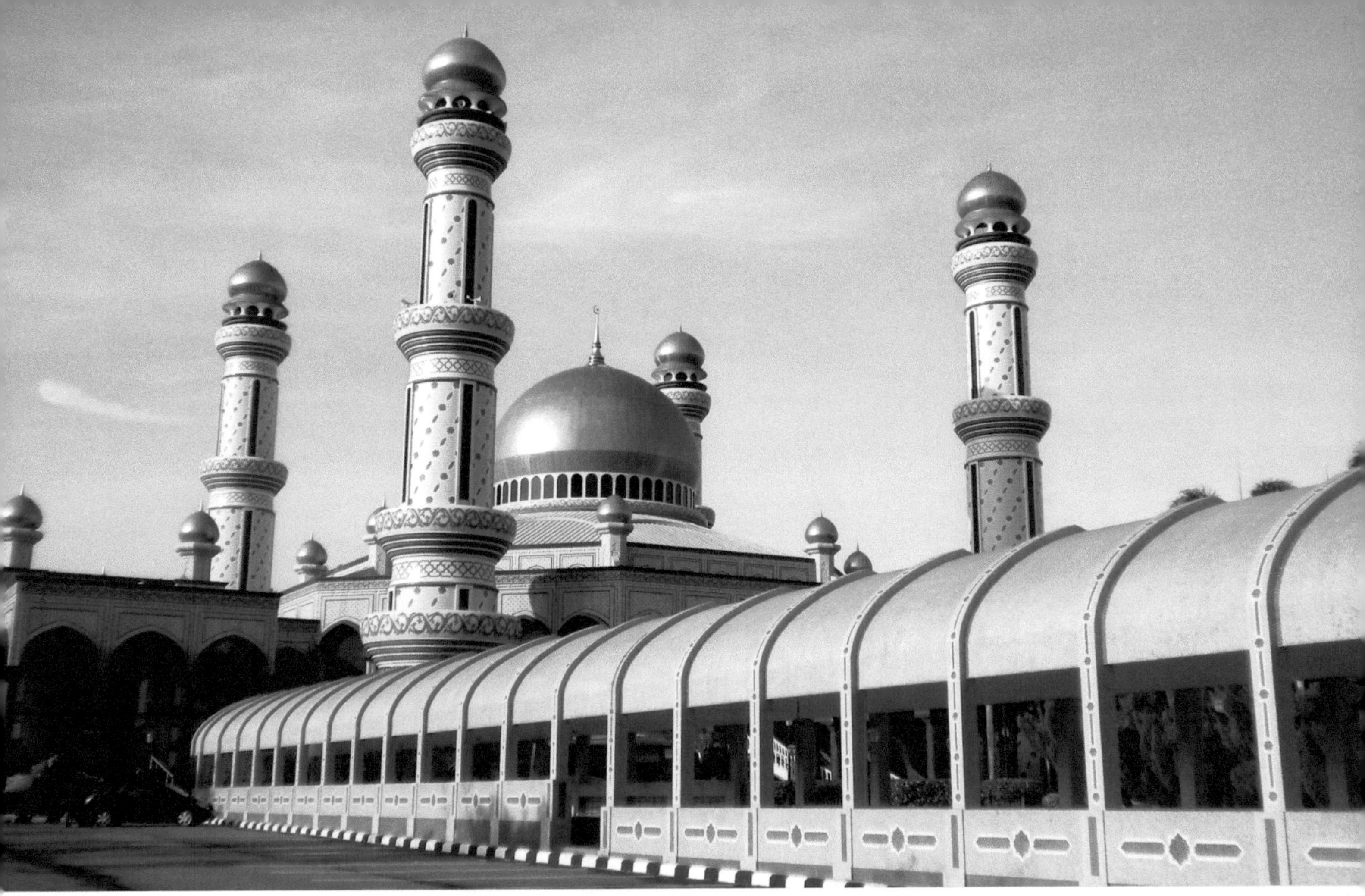

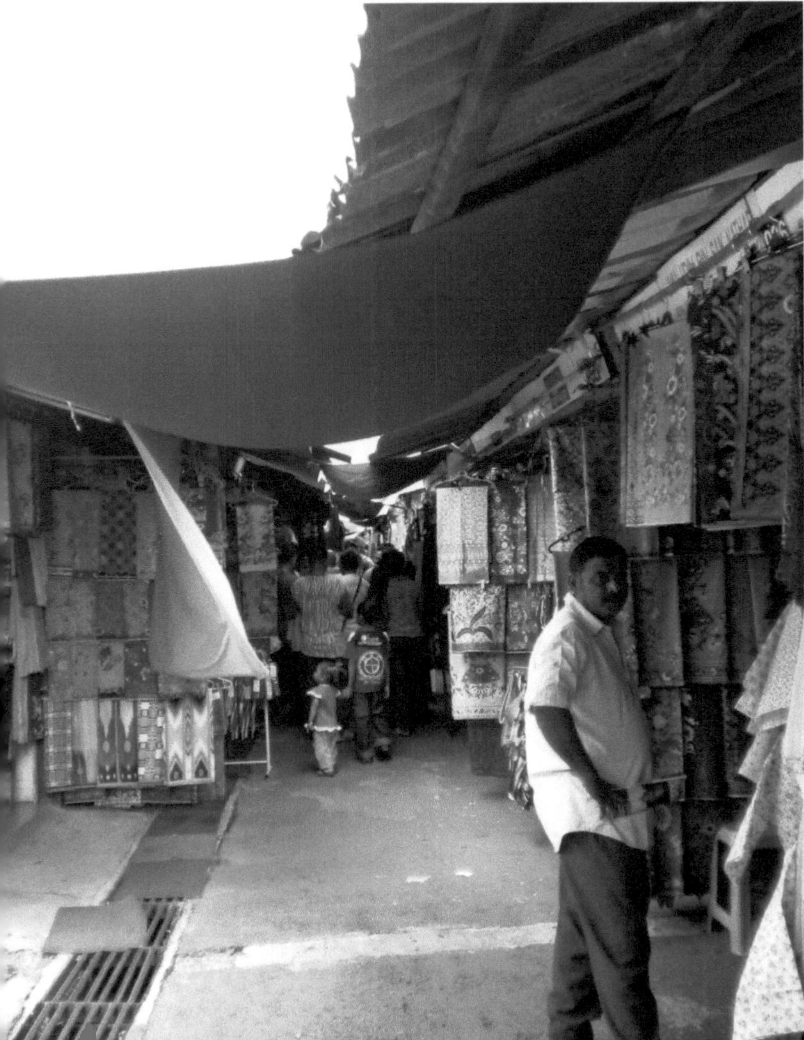

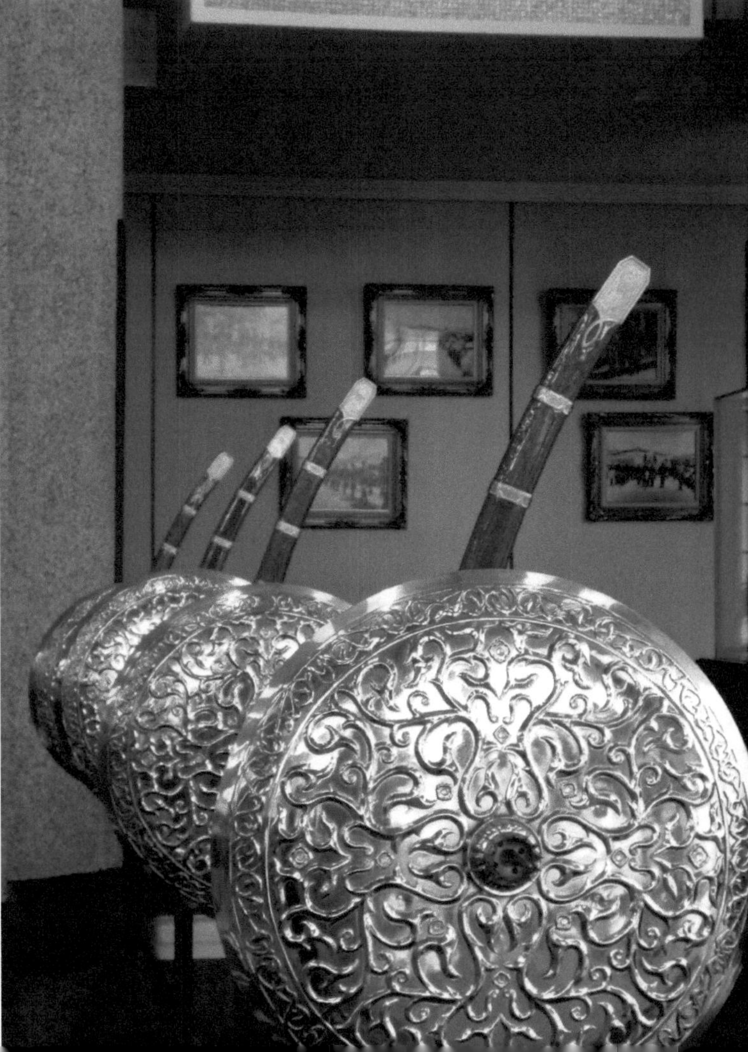

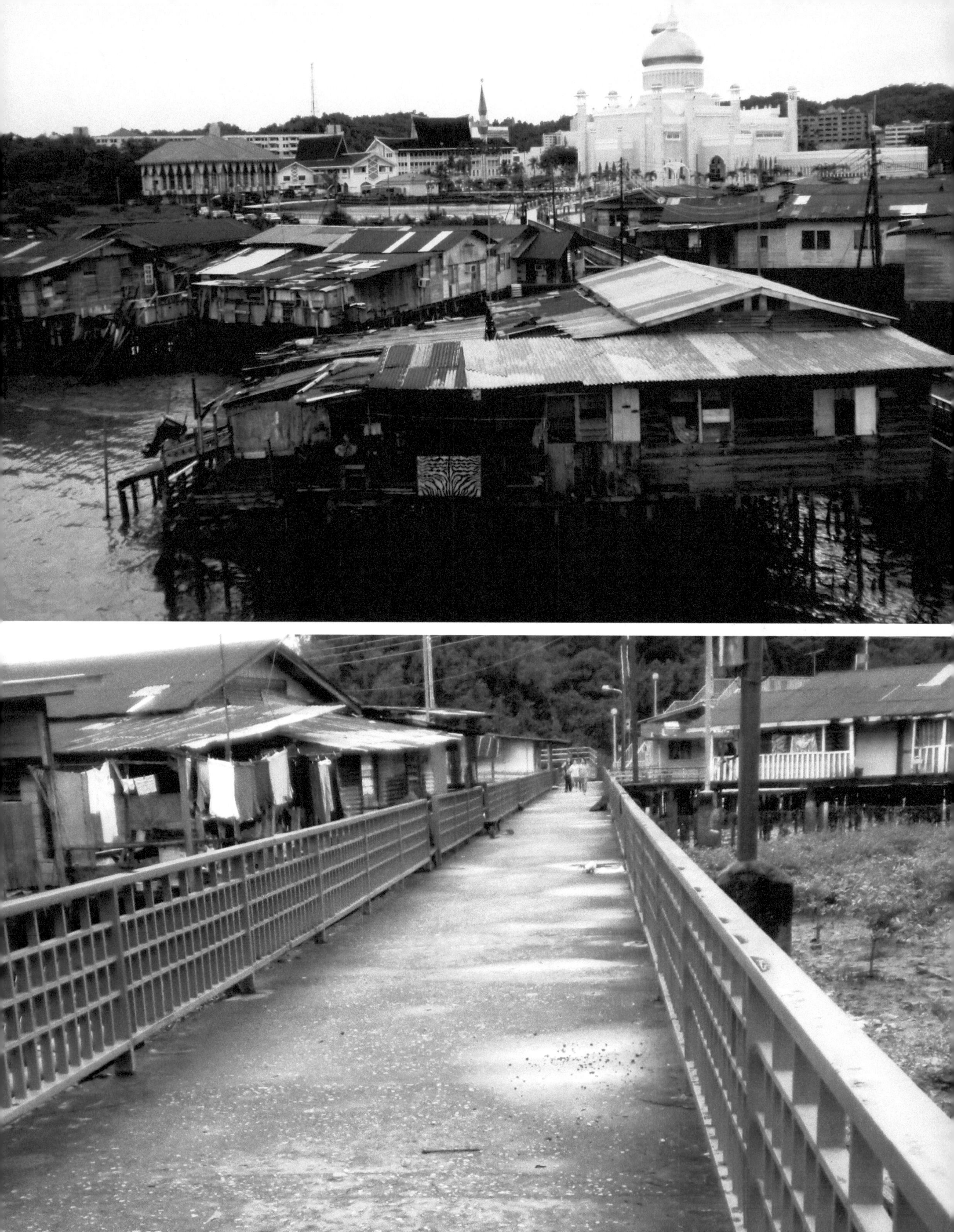

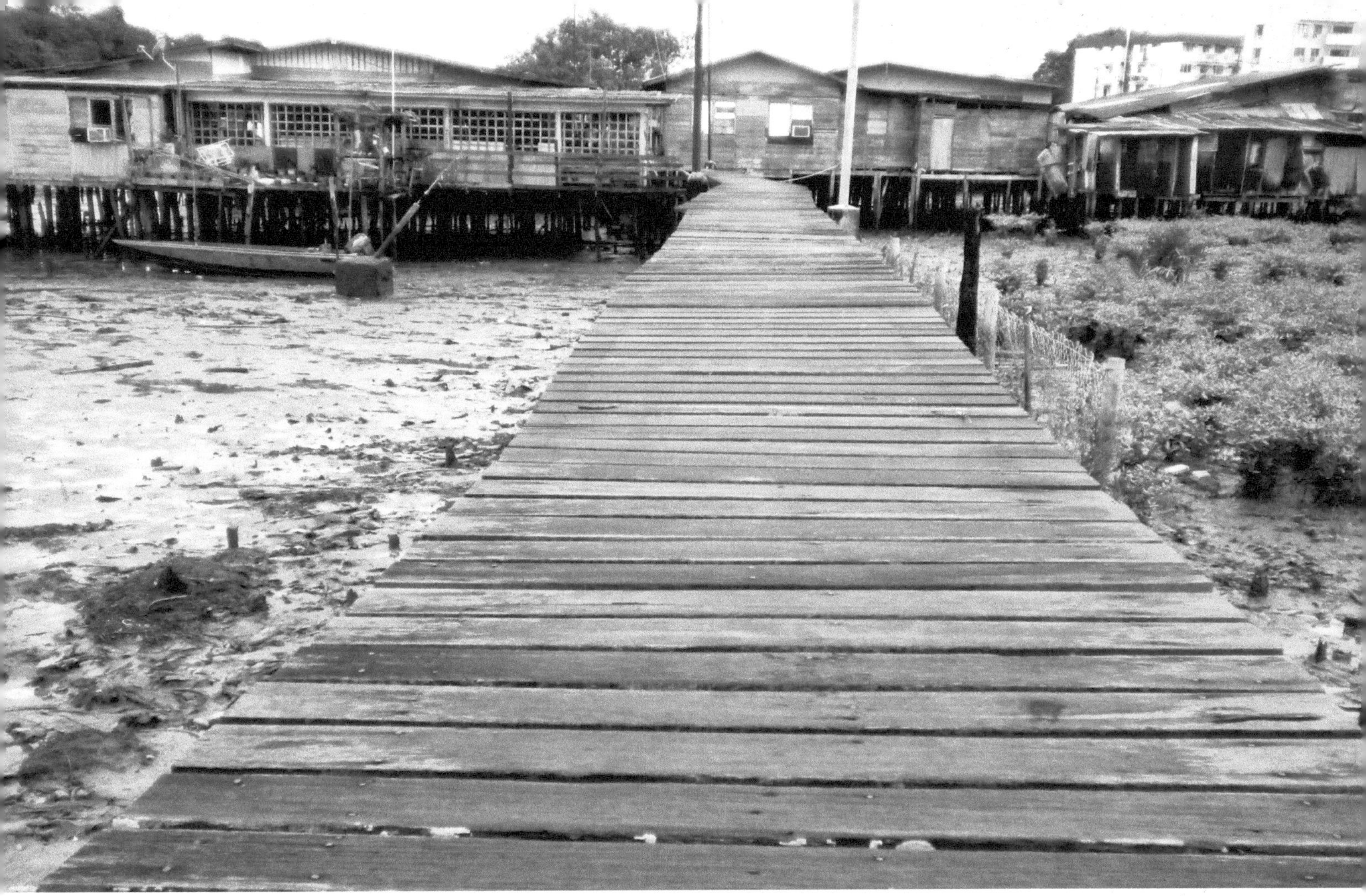

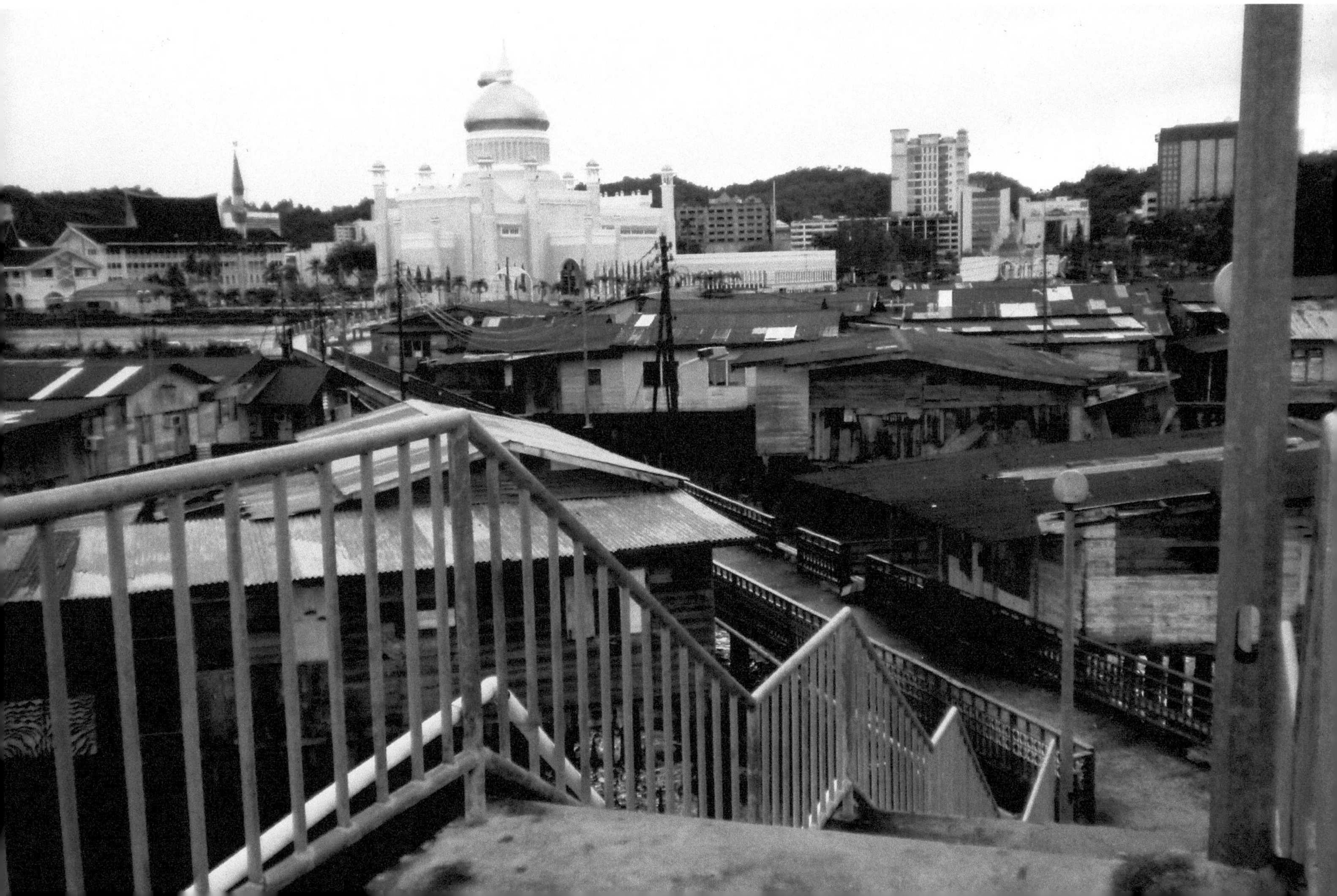

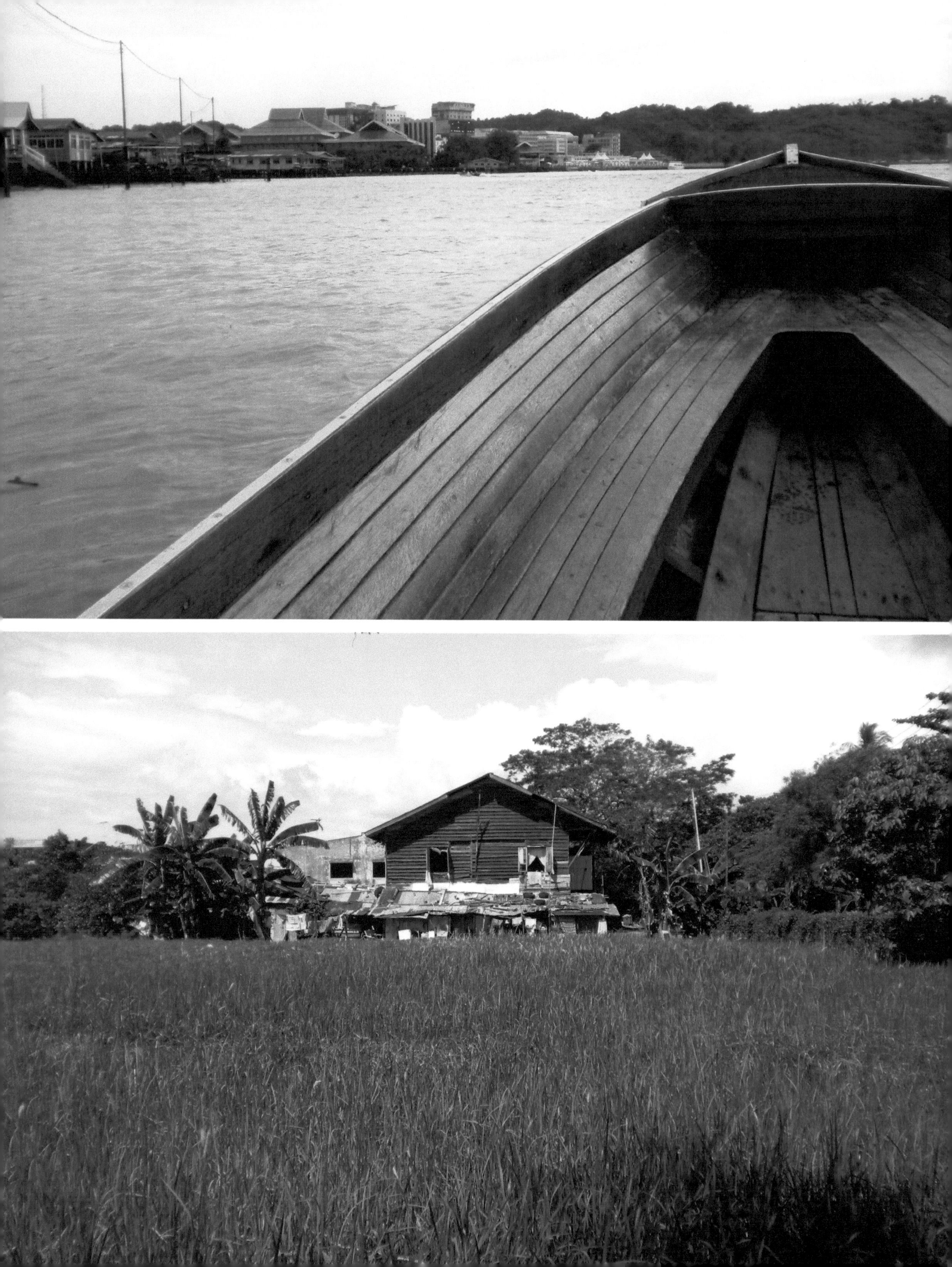

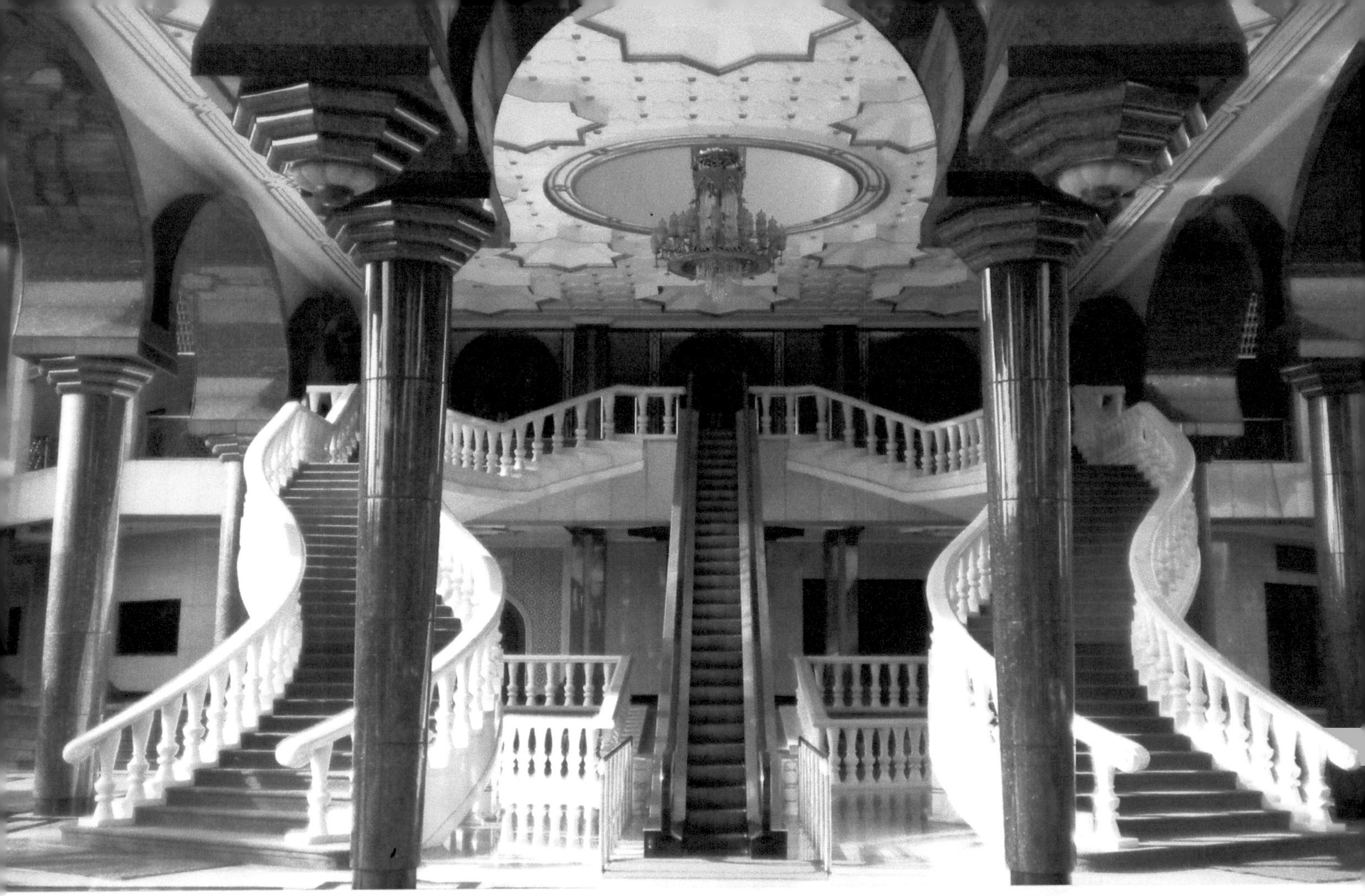

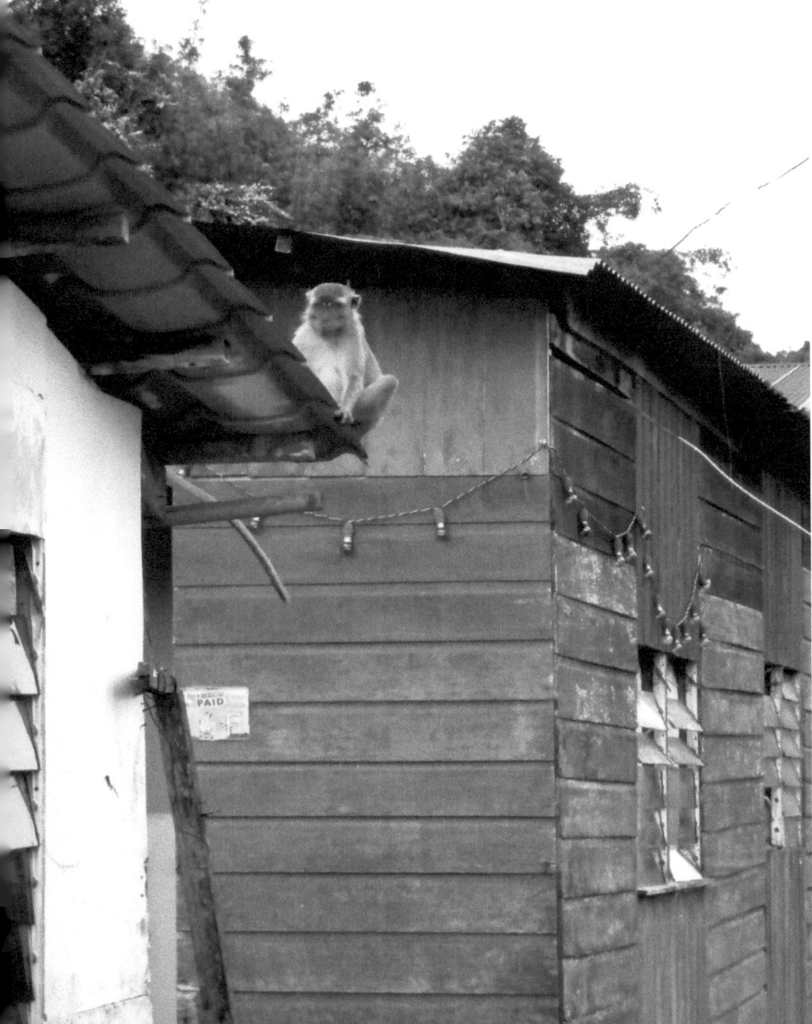
PAID

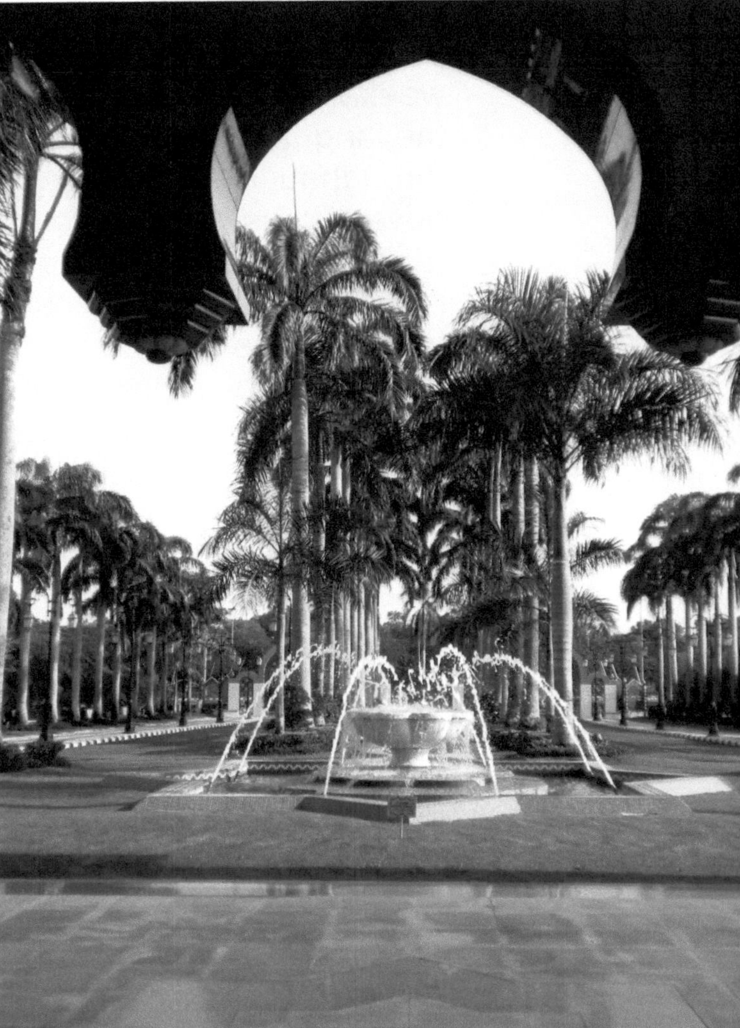

Addis Ababa, Ethiopia

The following photos were taken in Addis Ababa, Ethiopia and with great difficulty. I traveled to Ethiopia with a purpose, to transfer all of the US Embassy communications equipment from the old Embassy building to the new Embassy building. I stayed there for a month and was able to enjoy some of what Ethiopia has to offer. The country is large; there is a lot to see, being confined to only Addis Ababa, I did not see everything I wanted. This trip was my first to Africa so I was very excited. These photos were taken with a great degree of difficulty because of many factors. It was rainy season while I was there so it was constantly pouring, work kept me very busy even during weekends, and I lacked a thorough understanding of the language and how vastly everything is spread throughout that country. These factors made for many adventurous and wet days. The people there are eager to please and always greeted me with a smile. The food is delicious and inexpensive, the coffee there is a must try. I became addicted to the coffee and was upset with myself for not bringing any back to the US. The exchange rate is ridiculous! I was able to eat lunch and dinner combined for less than 10USD. If I have the chance to visit Ethiopia again, I will be prepared by bringing an umbrella and winter clothes.

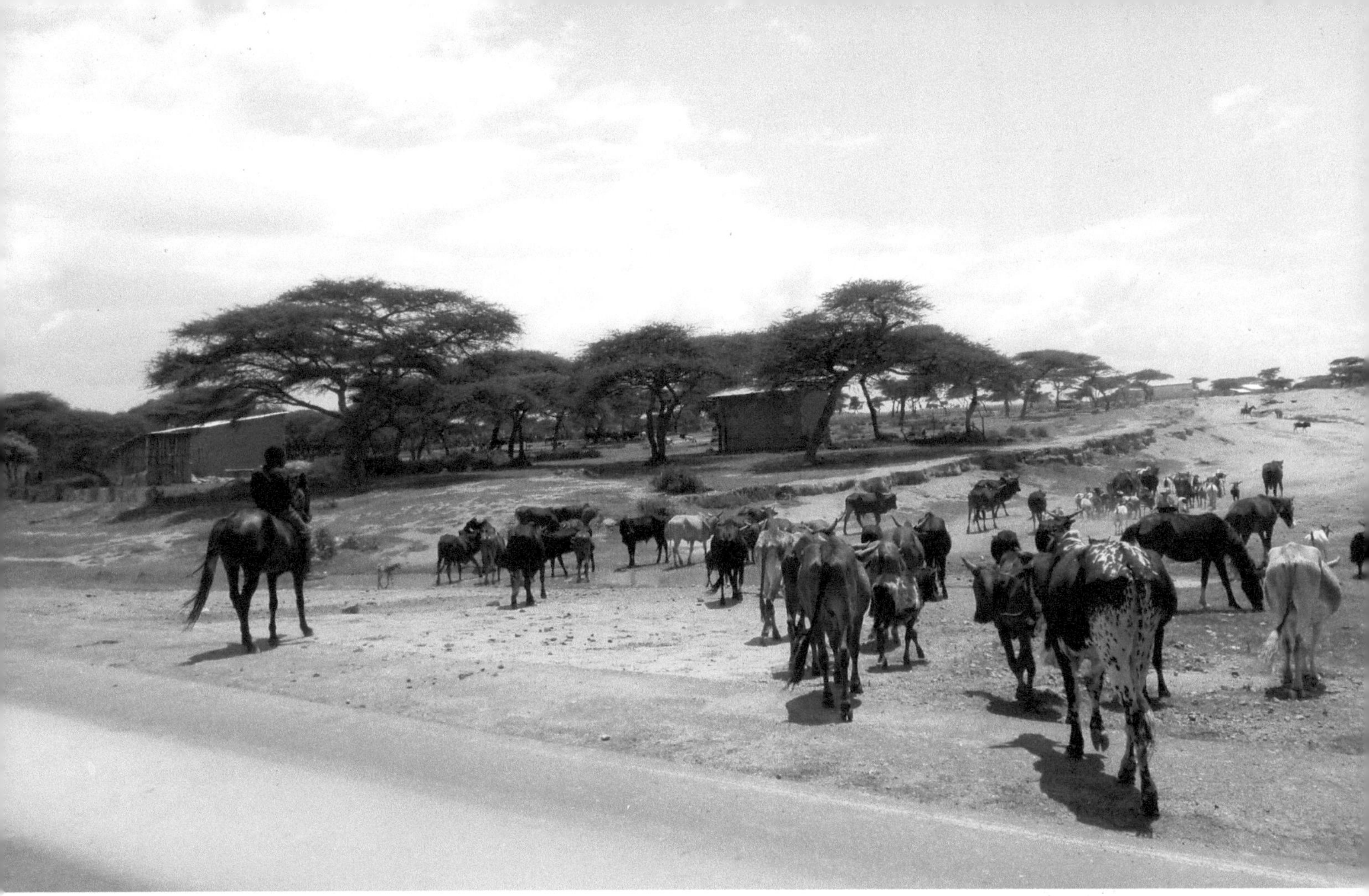

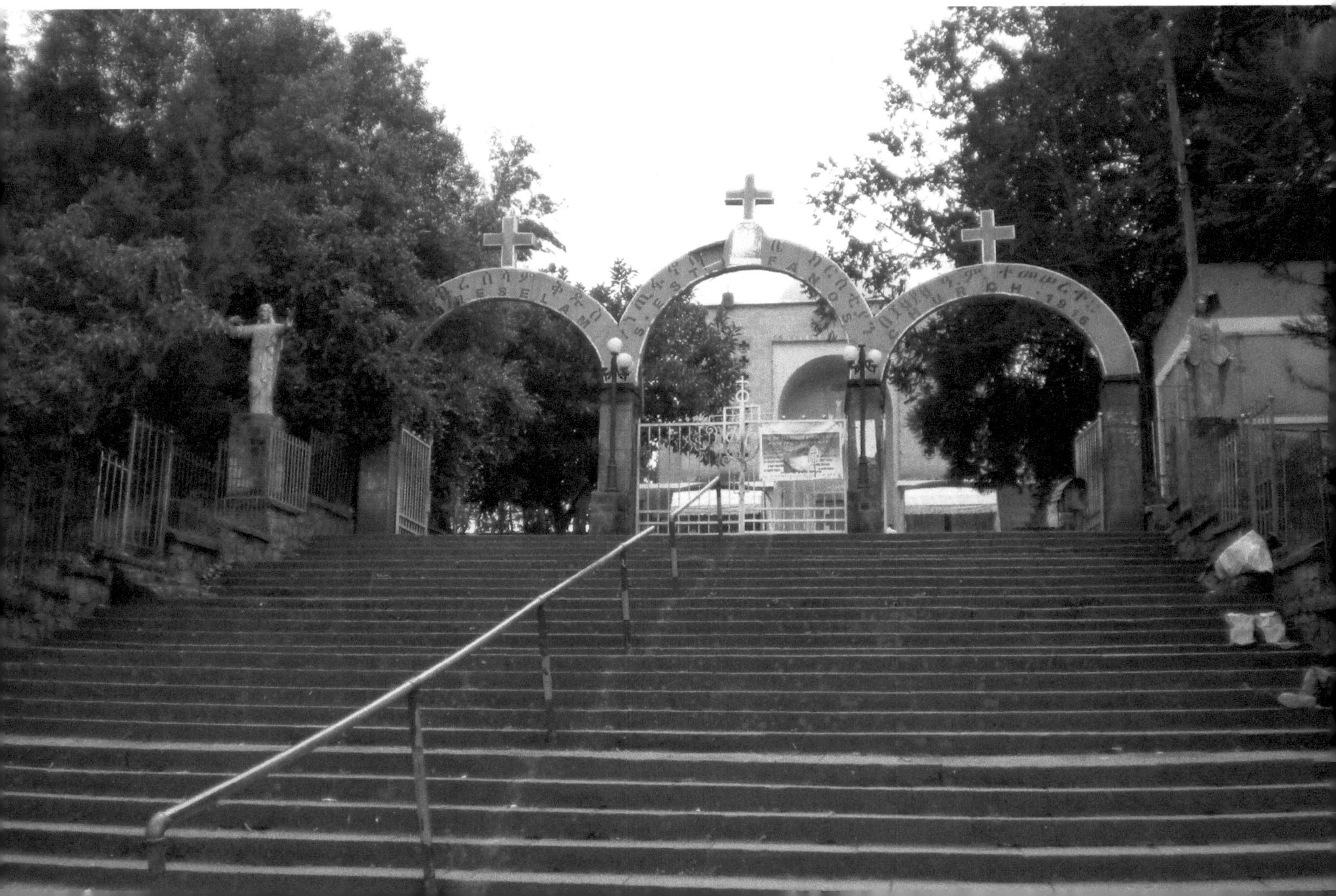

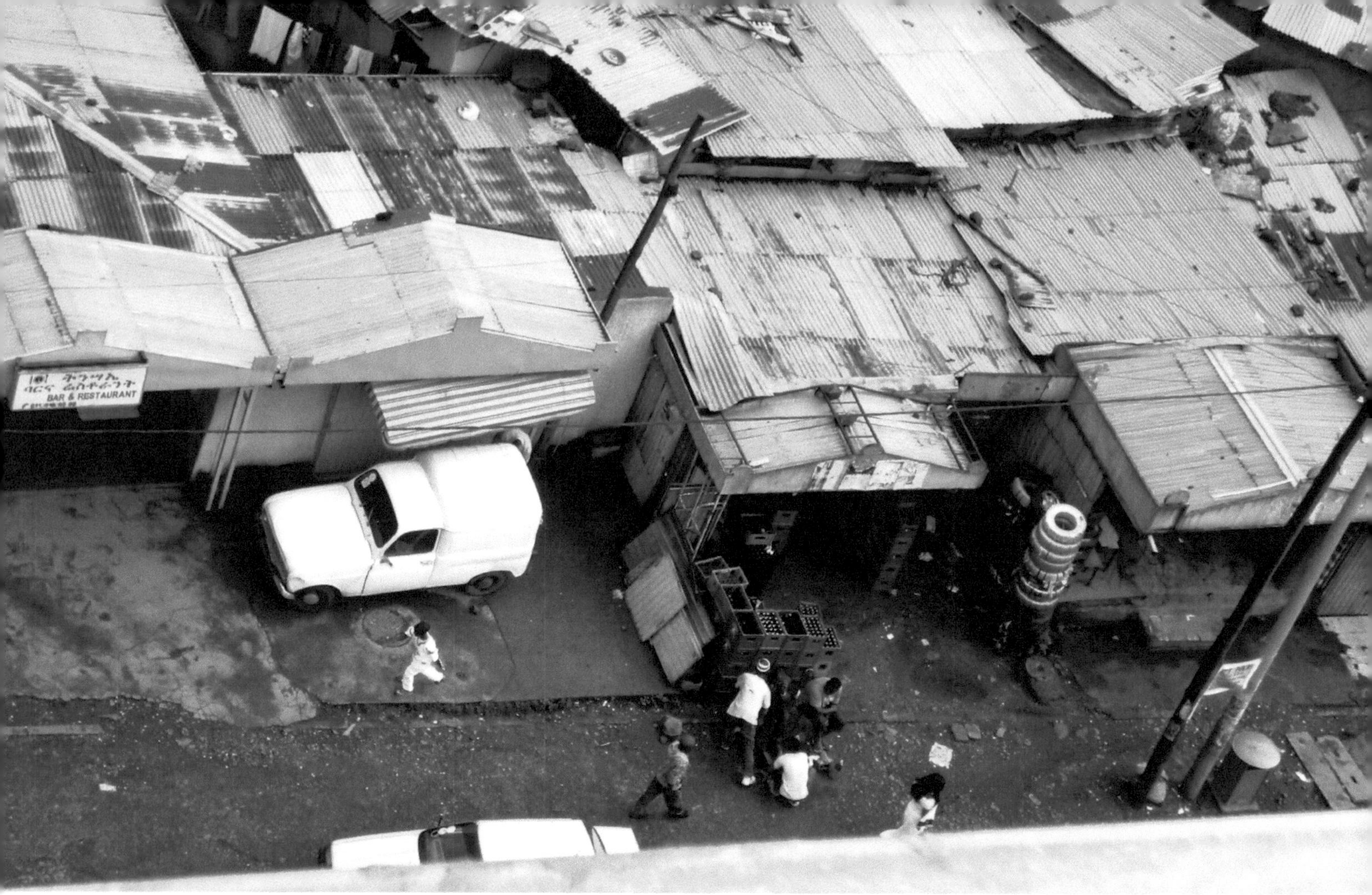

Read your Bible
one Chapter A-day
from Genesis.1 to Revelation.22.
Words of our beloved
PROPHET GAD

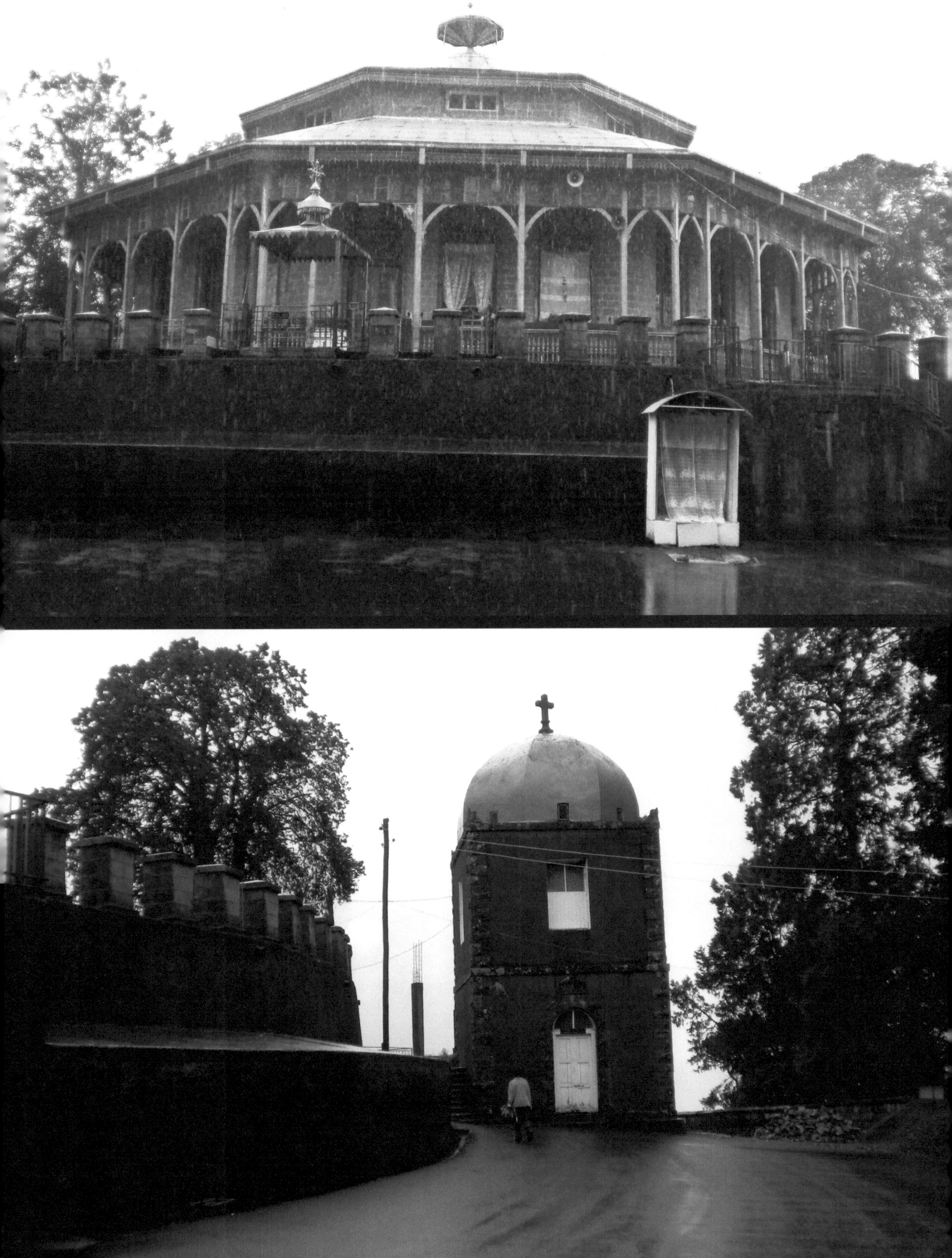

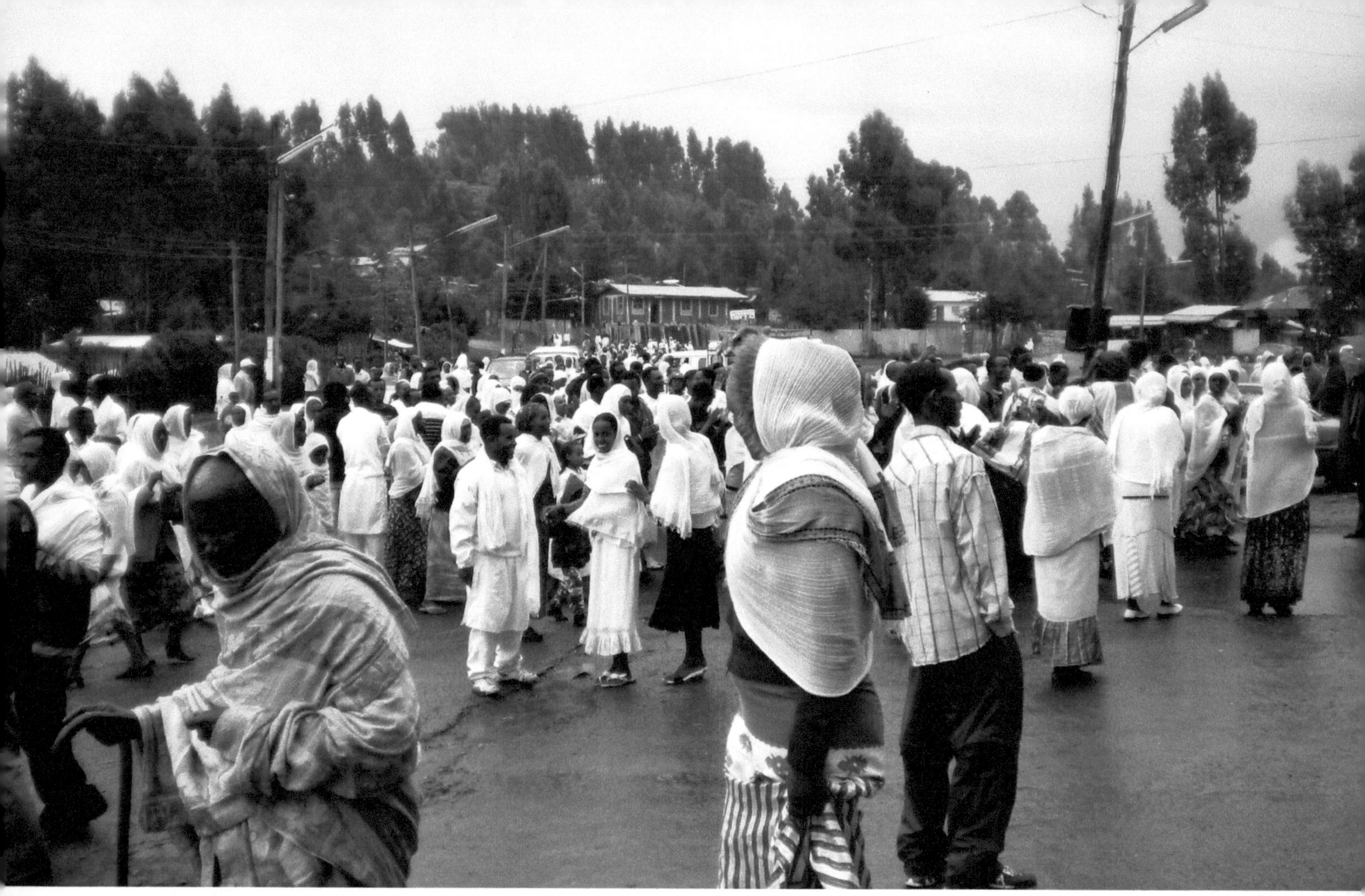

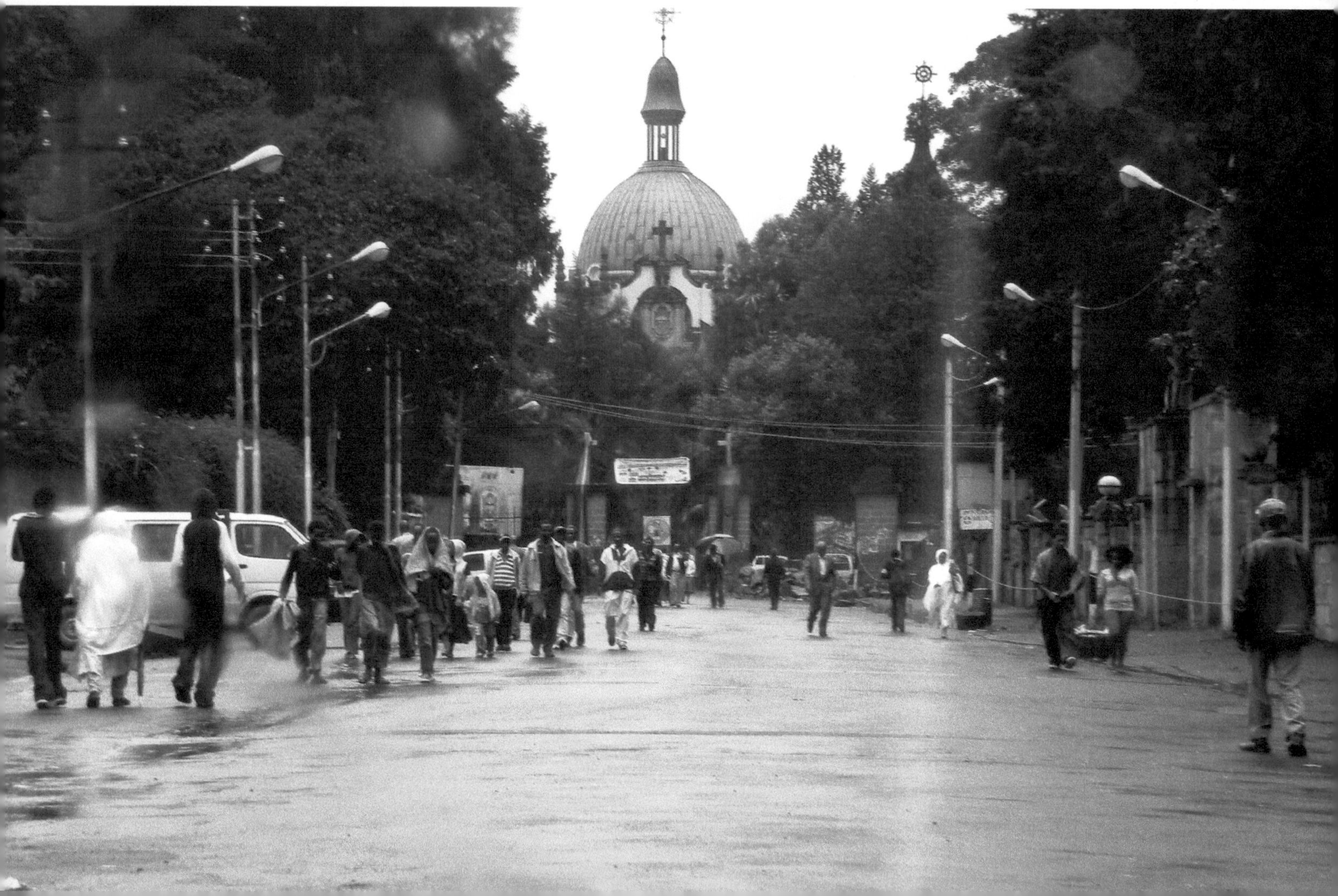

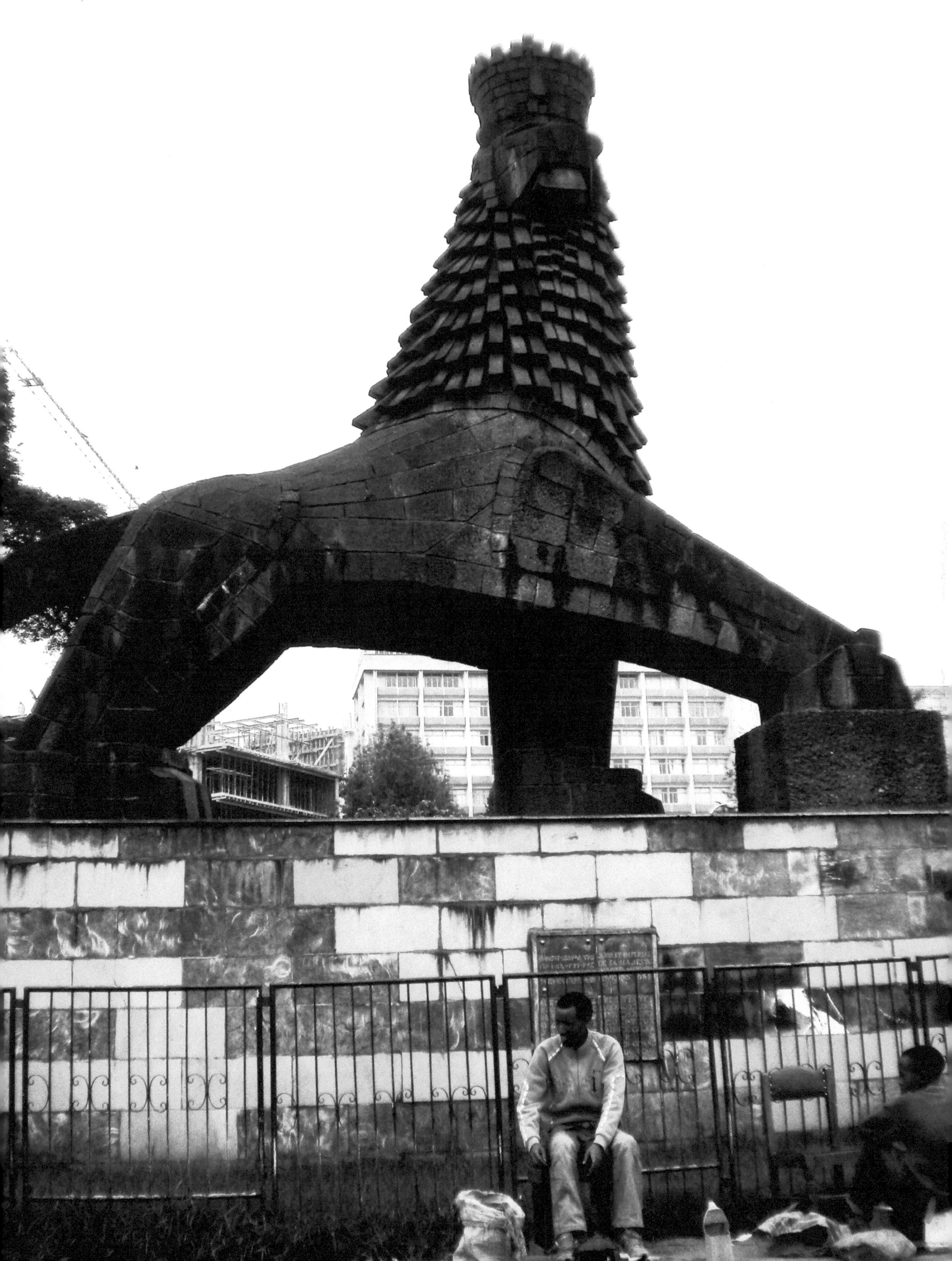

In Memorium

In memory of all those who lost their lives in the terrorist attacks on September 11, 2001, the US Embassy, in partnership with the Ethiopia Heritage Trust and in cooperation with the City Government of Addis Ababa and the Government of Ethiopia has planted three thousand (3000) indigenous seedlings to mark the beginning of the Ethiopia-America September 11 Memorial Park.

Dedicated this day, September 10, 2004

by Ambassador Aurelia E. Brazeal and Mayor Arkebe Oquba in the presence of His Excellency President Girma Wolde-Giorgis

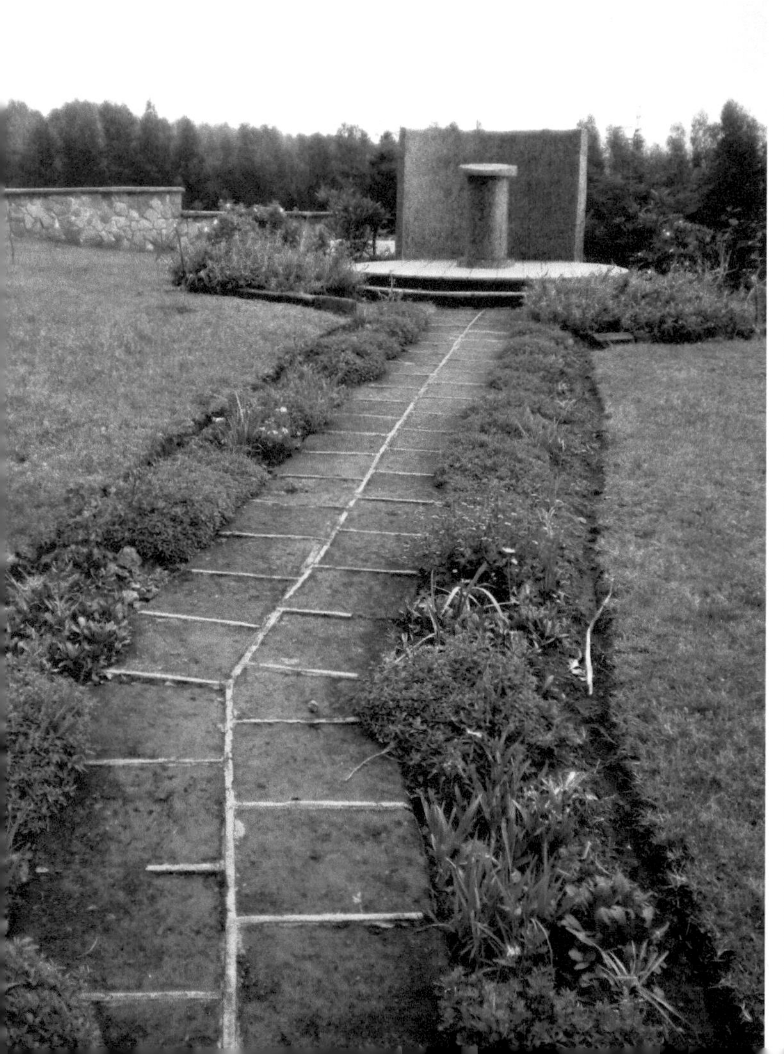

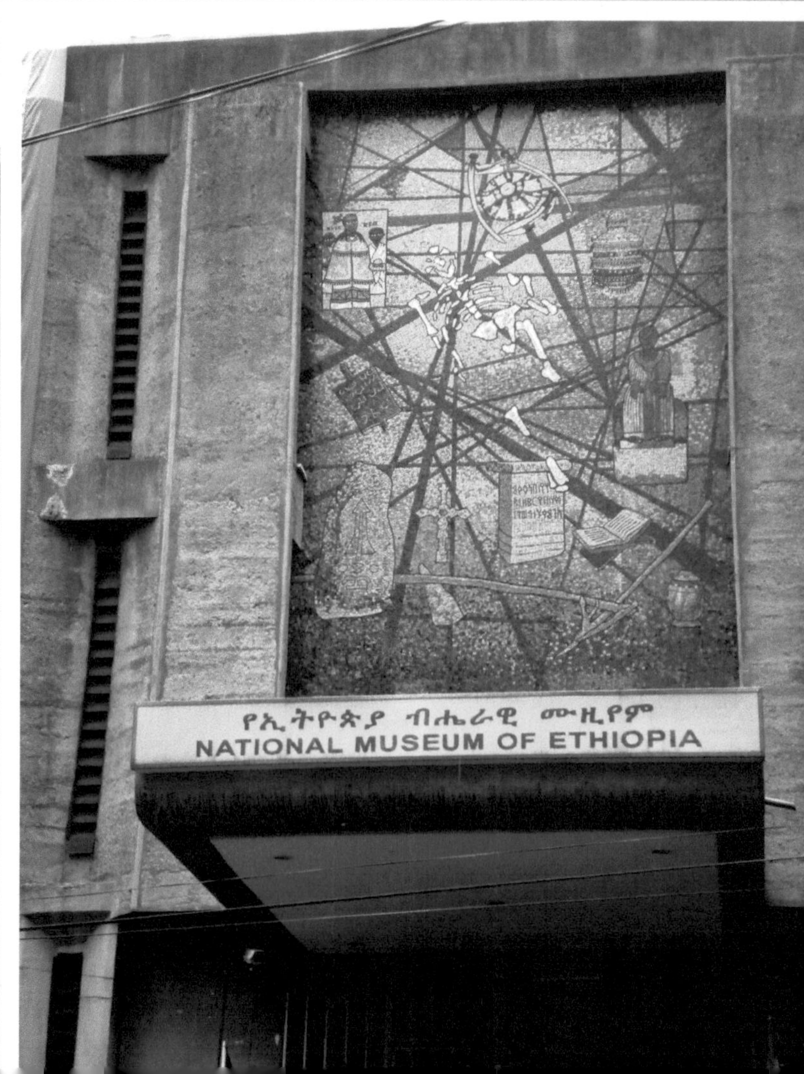

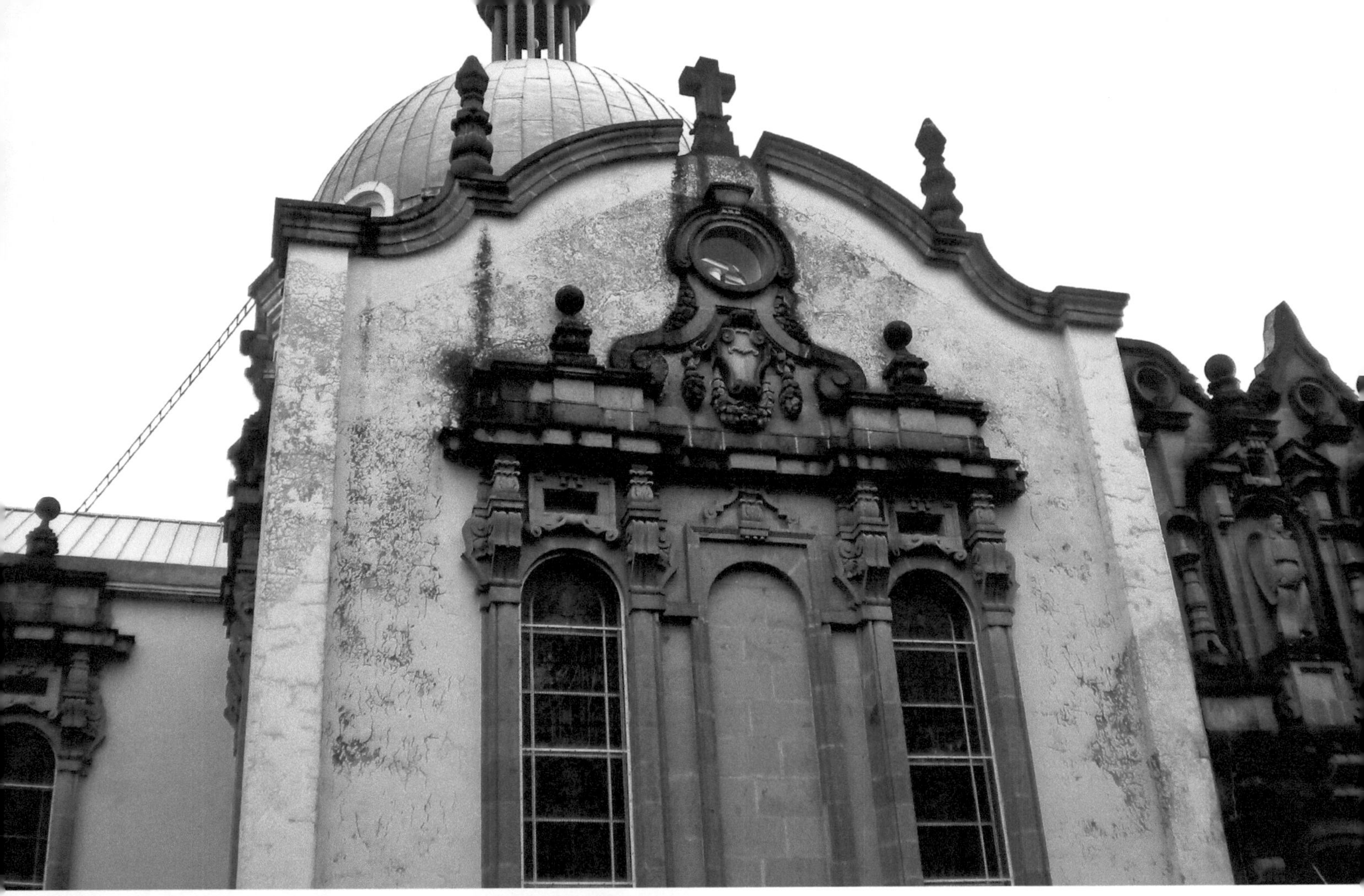

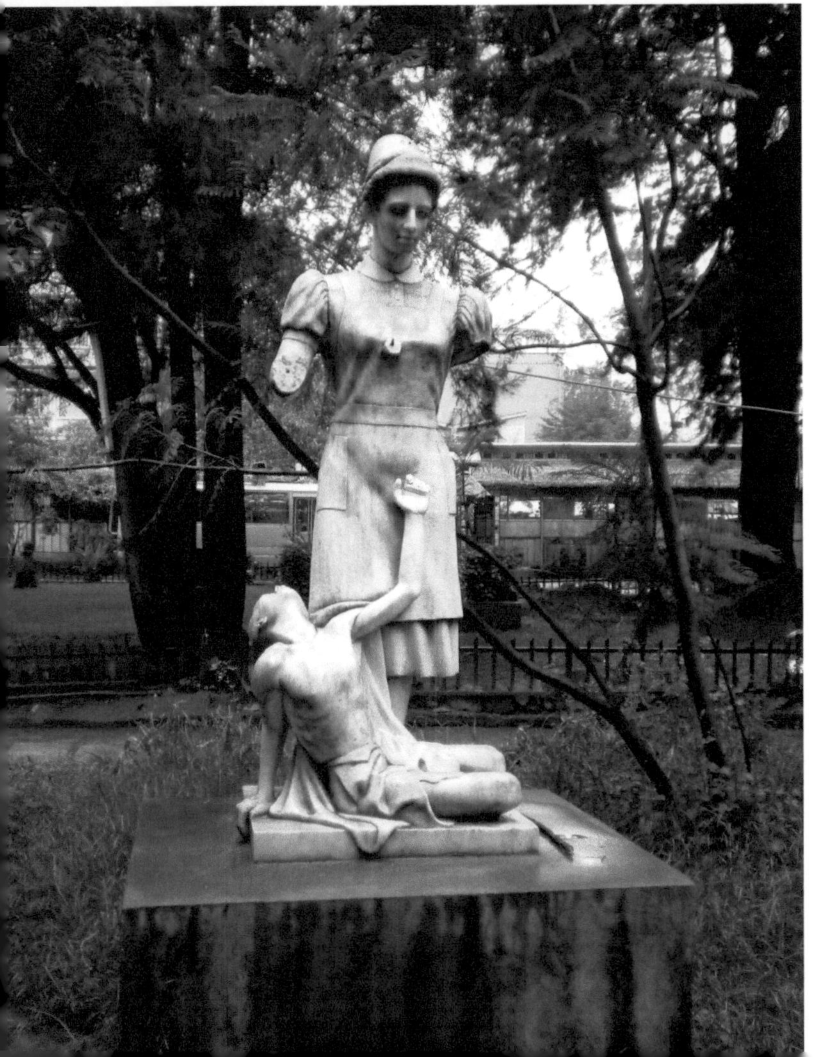

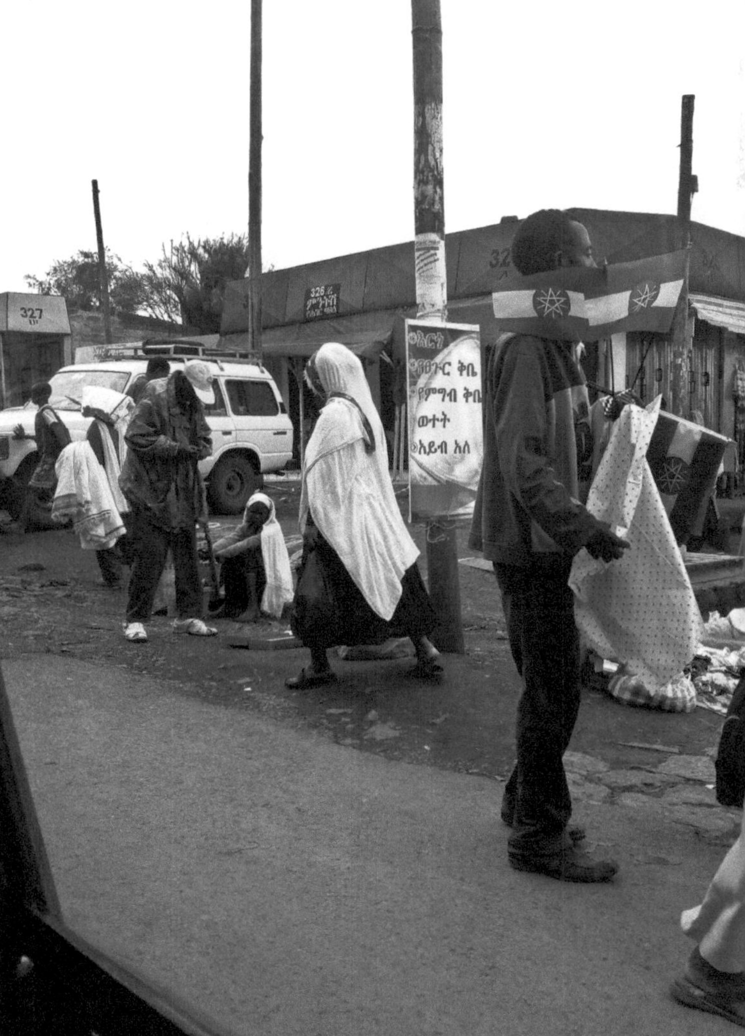
327
326
እርጎ
ፀጉር ቅቤ
የምግብ ቅቤ
ወተት
አይብ አለ

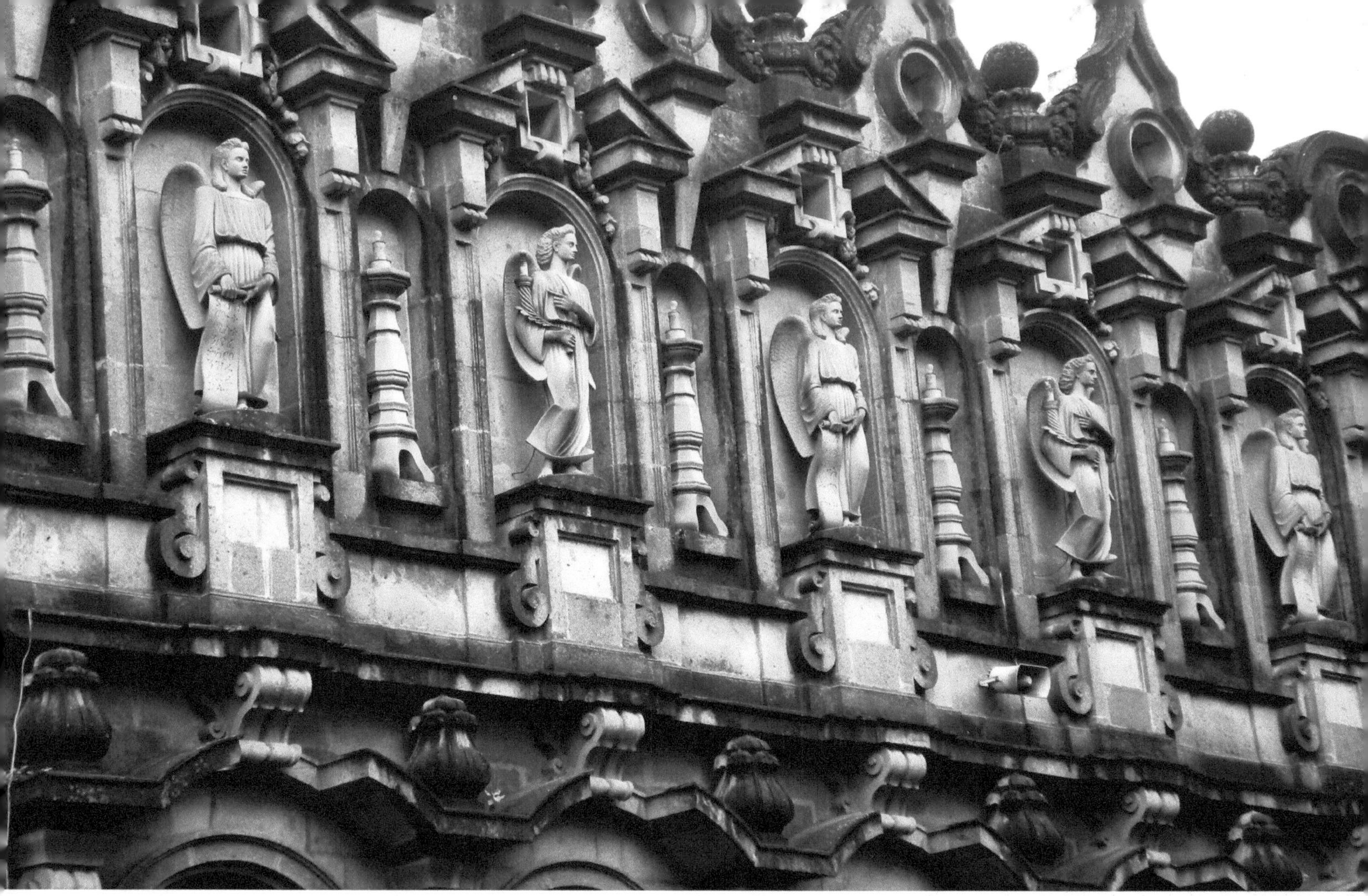

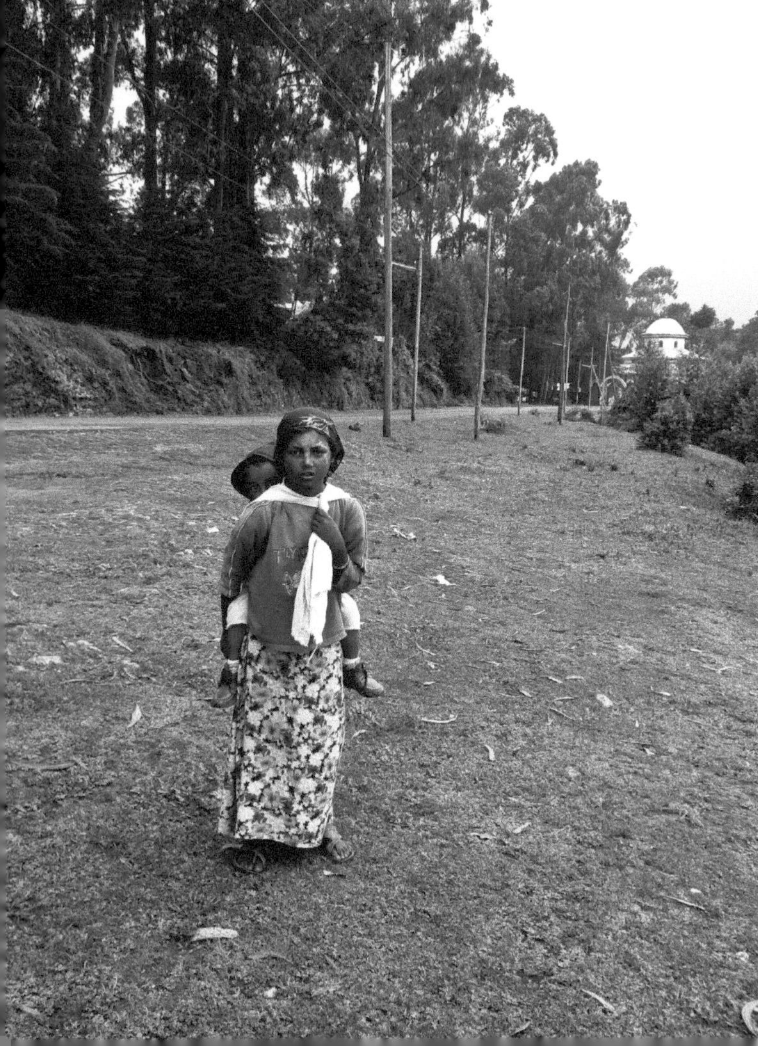

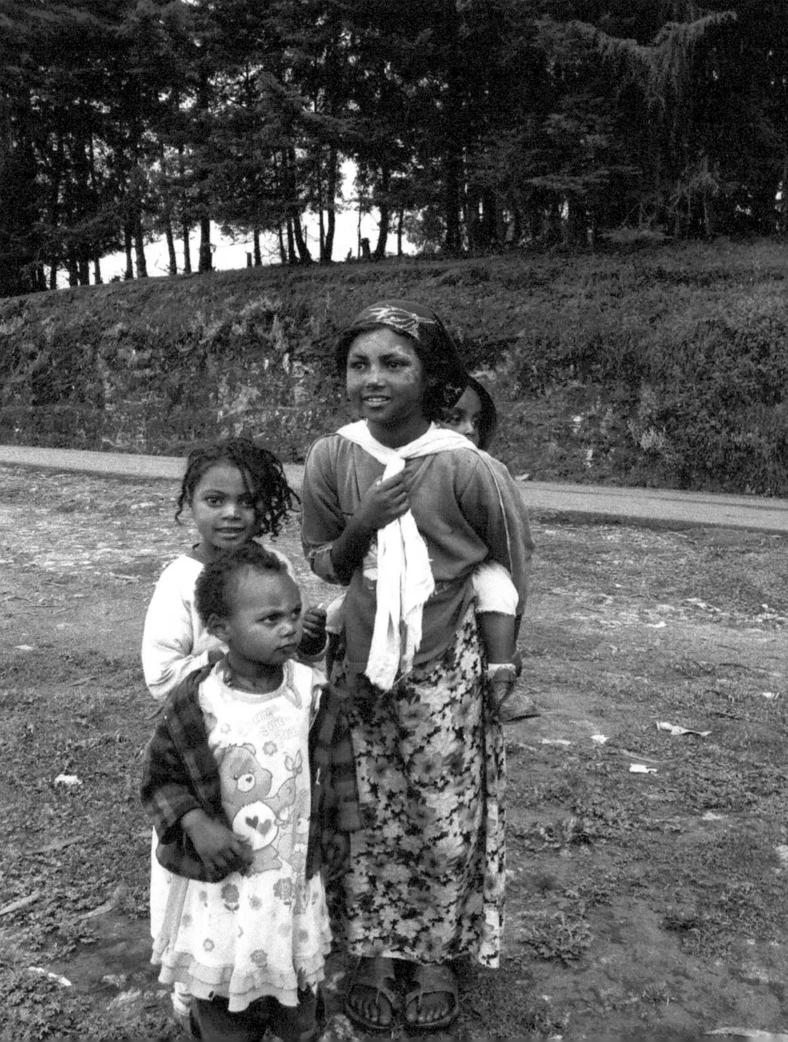

Luxembourg, The Grand Duchy of Luxembourg

The following photos are from Luxembourg, The Grand Duchy of Luxembourg, it certainly was grand. My hotel was in the middle of downtown, so picture taking opportunities were abundant. This trip was incredibly enjoyable and it was my first time in Europe. My purpose in Luxembourg was to upgrade some of the network cables that were in the US Embassy. I worked in Luxembourg for a month and a half. Luxembourg is not a large country so there was plenty of time to explore the city and the countryside. Common things like food, clothing and transportation were expensive due to the exchange rate of the US dollar compared to the stronger euro, food was great and; people tended to keep to themselves and did not pay much attention to me. There were plenty of great sites to see, castles are abundant, and the underground casement, which is a labyrinth of defensive passageways under the city, was spectacular. Luxembourg is the first country I visited in Europe and it definitely won't be the last.

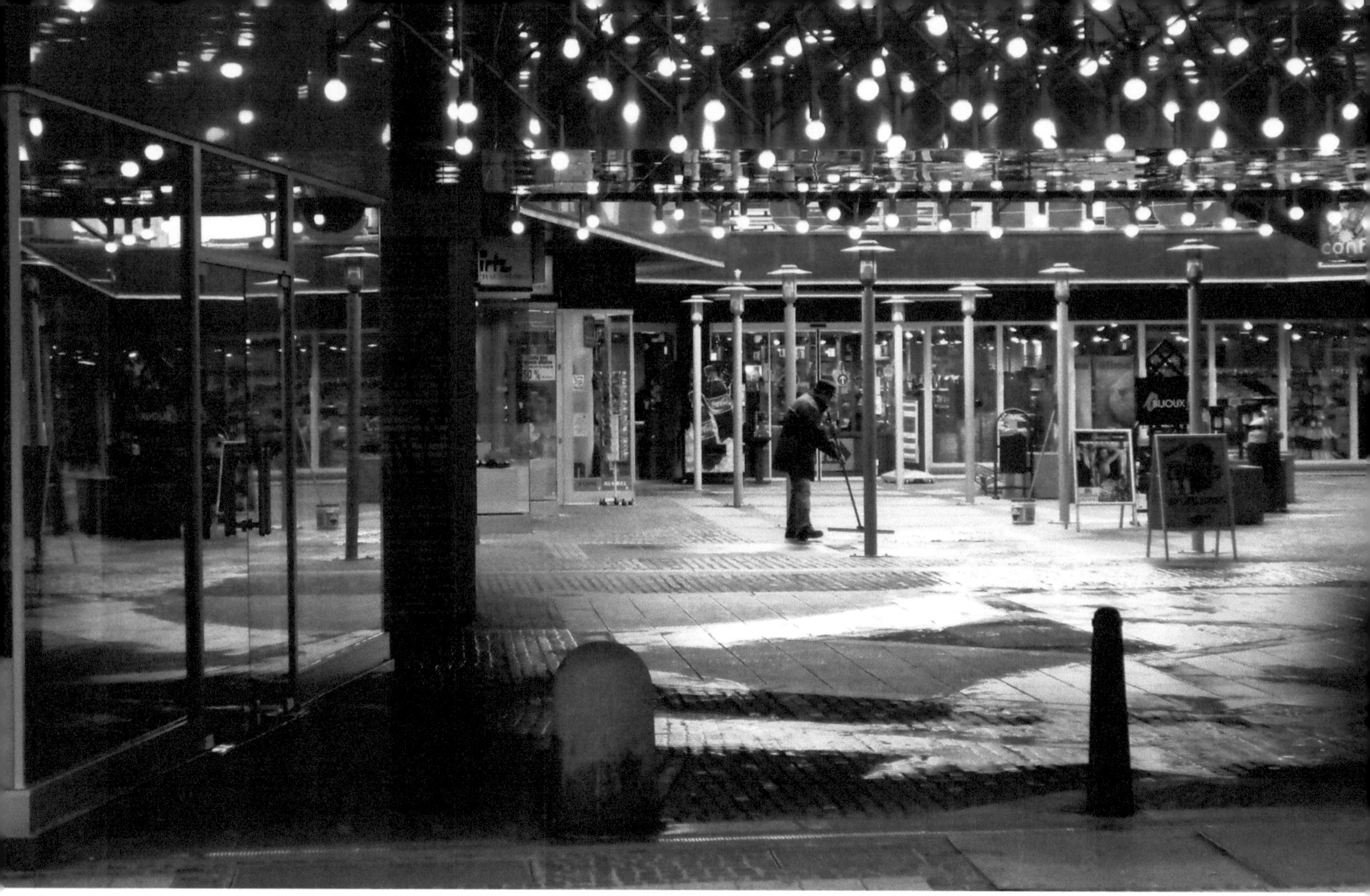

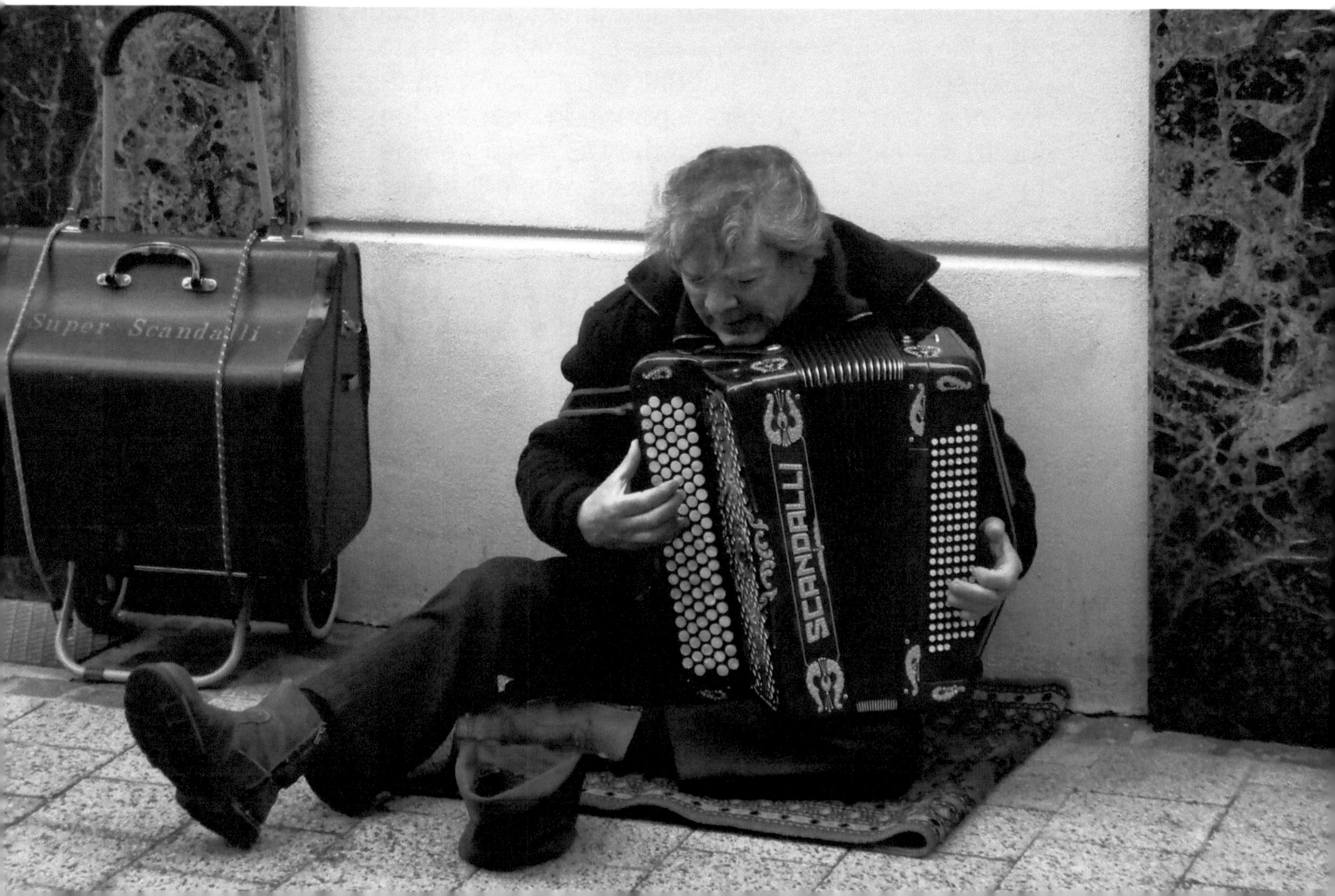
Super Scandalli
SCANDALLI

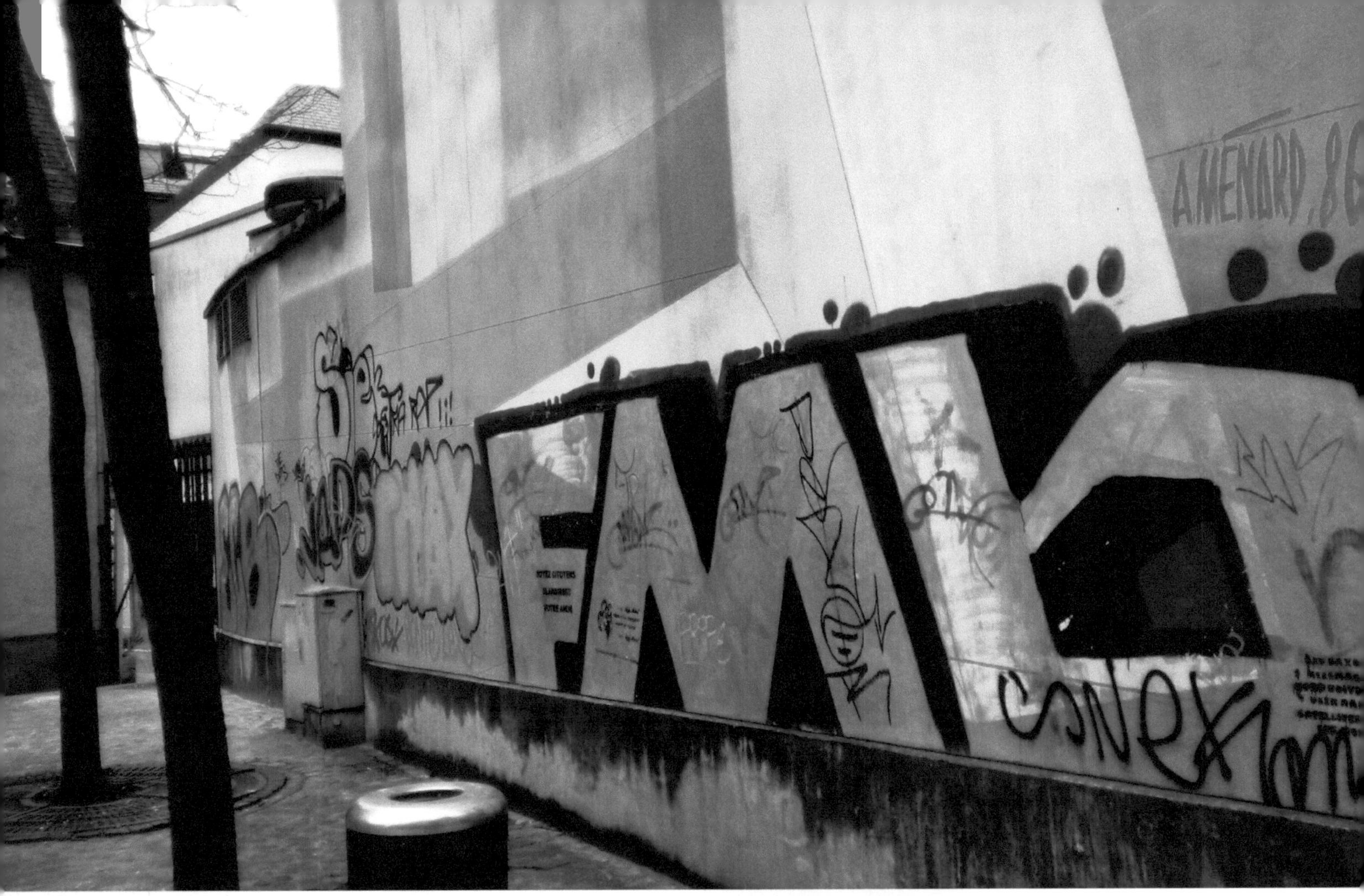

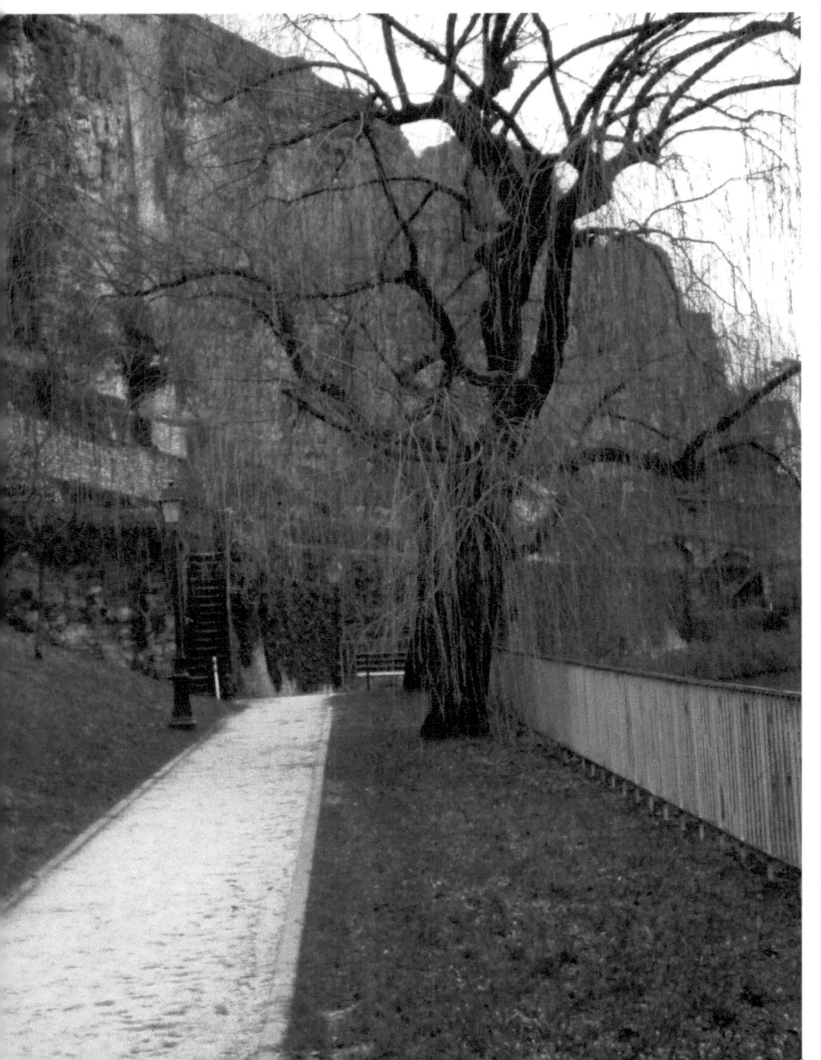

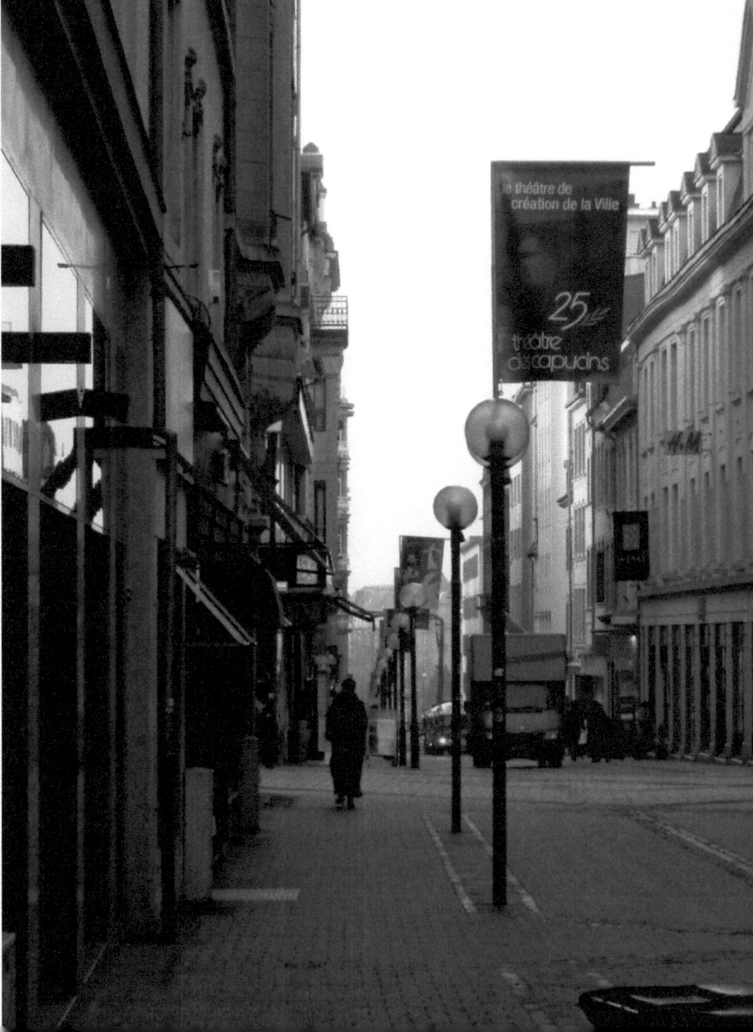
le théatre de
création de la Ville
25
théâtre des capucins

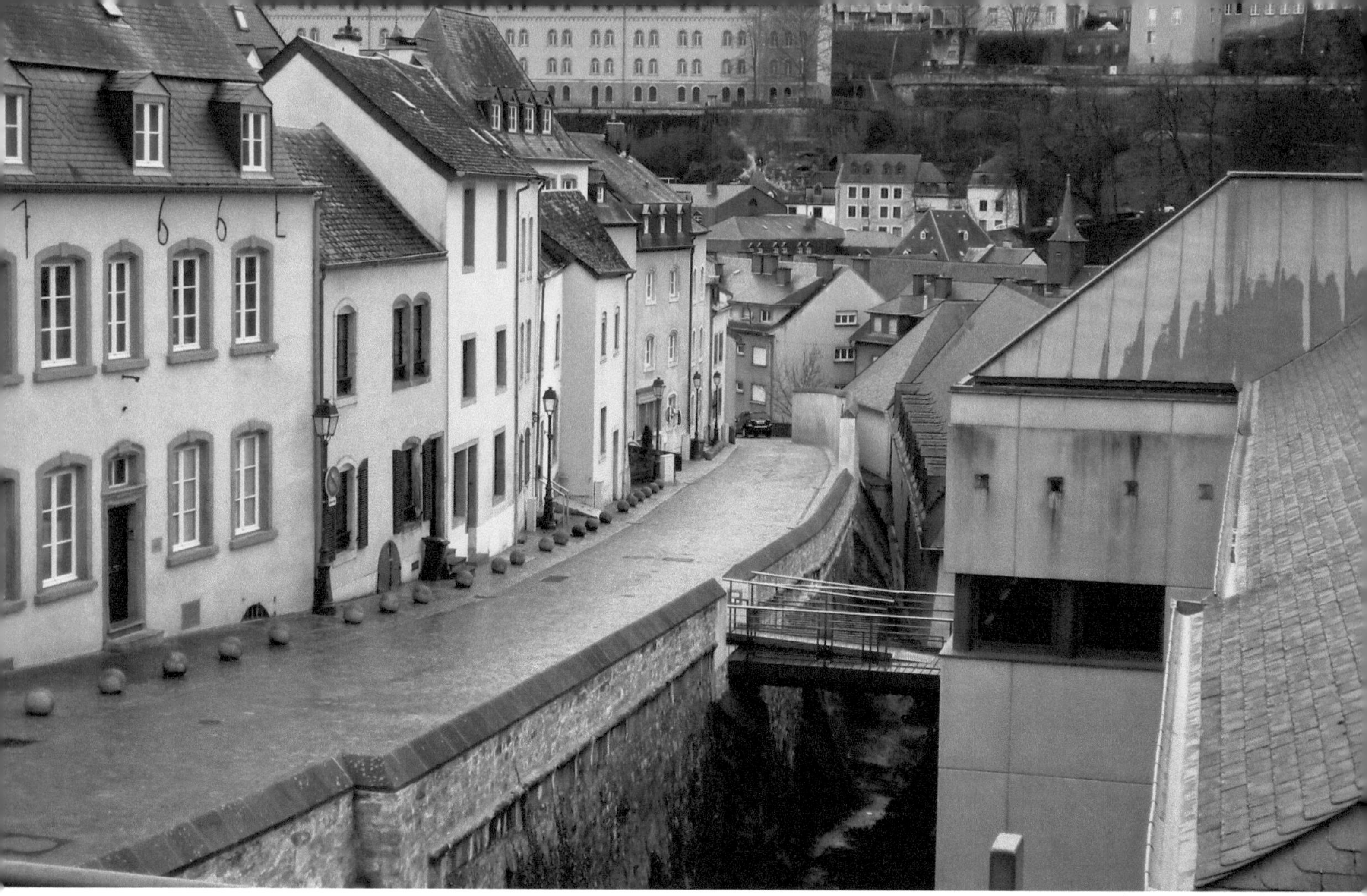

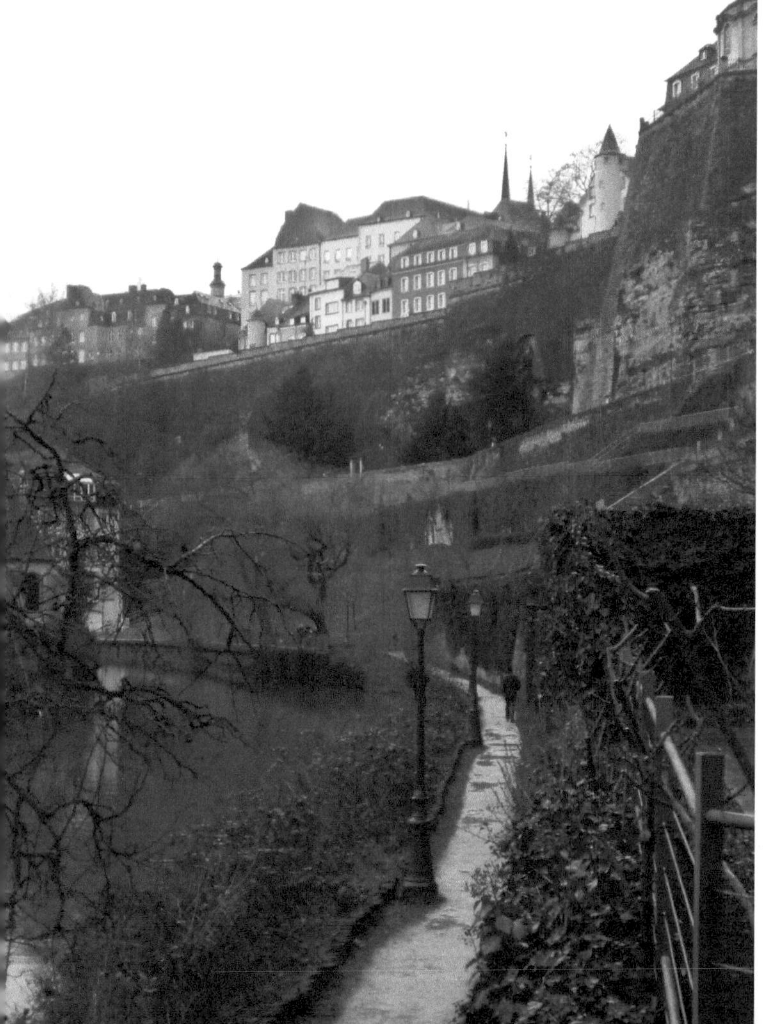

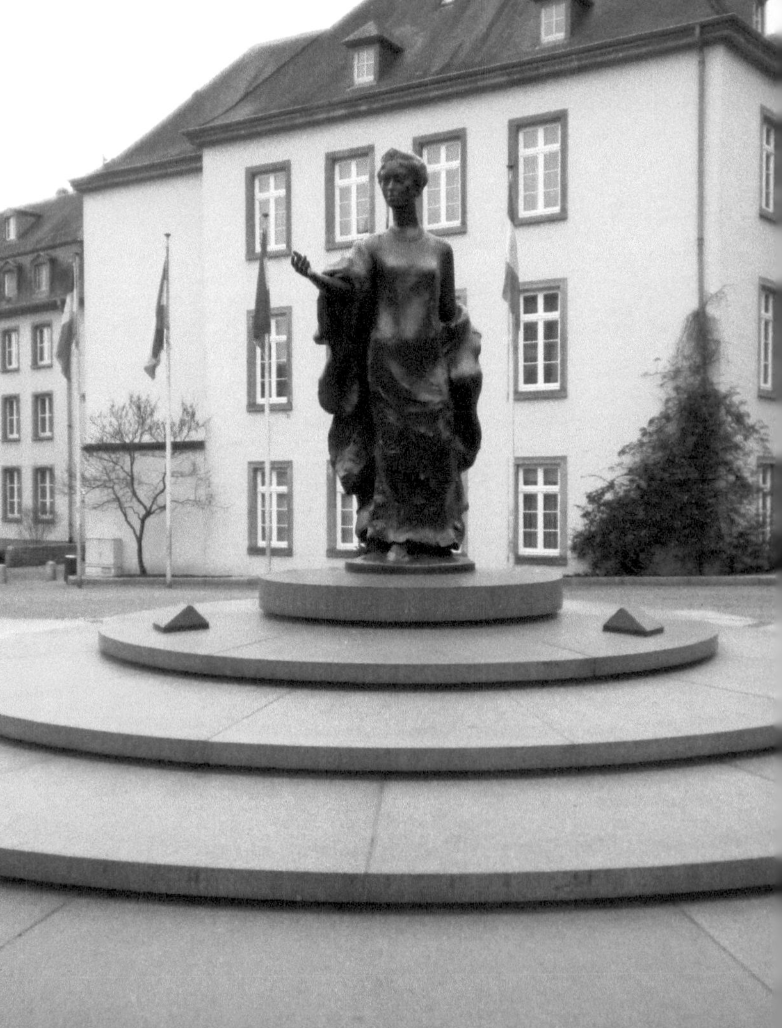

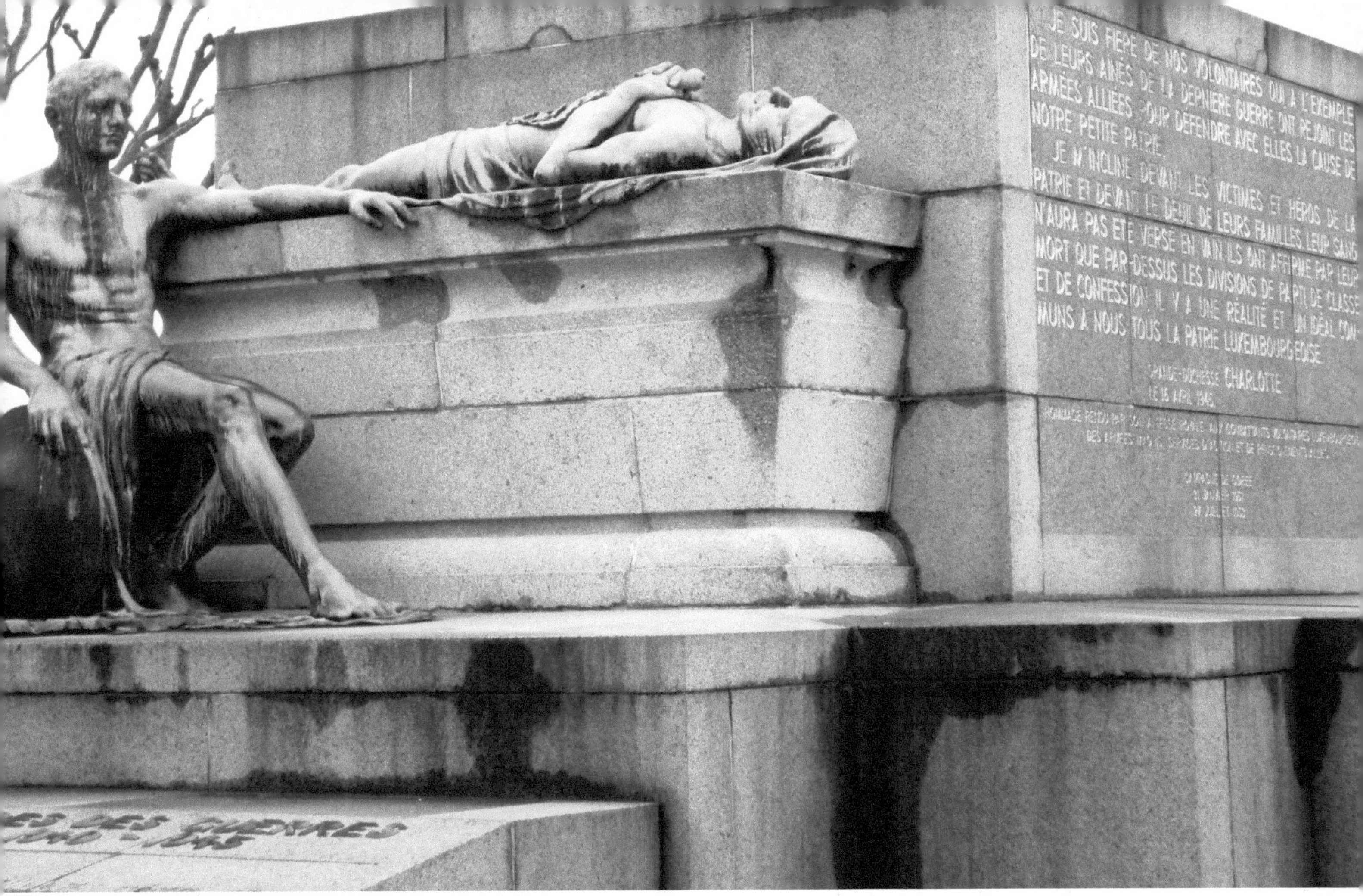

JE SUIS FIÈRE DE NOS VOLONTAIRES QUI A L'EXEMPLE DE LEURS AINÉS DE LA DERNIÈRE GUERRE ONT REJOINT LES ARMÉES ALLIÉES POUR DÉFENDRE AVEC ELLES LA CAUSE DE NOTRE PETITE PATRIE.
JE M'INCLINE DEVANT LES VICTIMES ET HÉROS DE LA PATRIE ET DEVANT LE DEUIL DE LEURS FAMILLES. LEUR SANG N'AURA PAS ÉTÉ VERSÉ EN VAIN. ILS ONT AFFIRMÉ PAR LEUR MORT QUE PAR-DESSUS LES DIVISIONS DE PARTI DE CLASSE ET DE CONFESSION IL Y A UNE RÉALITÉ ET UN IDÉAL COMMUNS À NOUS TOUS LA PATRIE LUXEMBOURGEOISE.
GRANDE-DUCHESSE CHARLOTTE
LE 16 AVRIL 1945

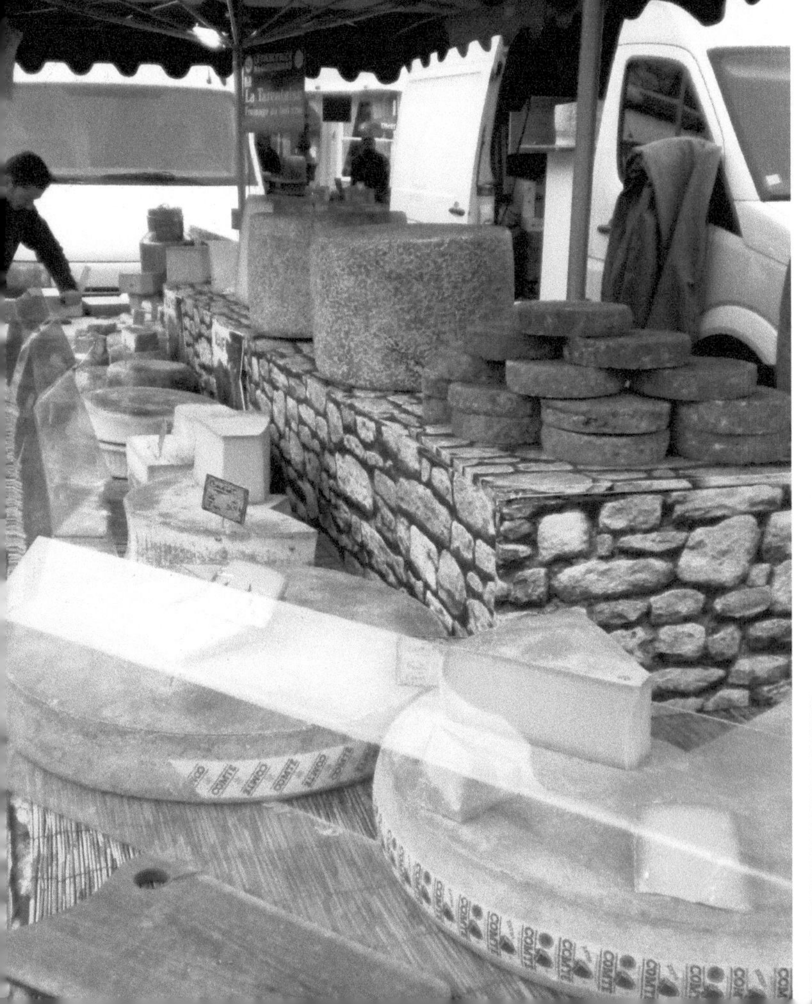
COMTE

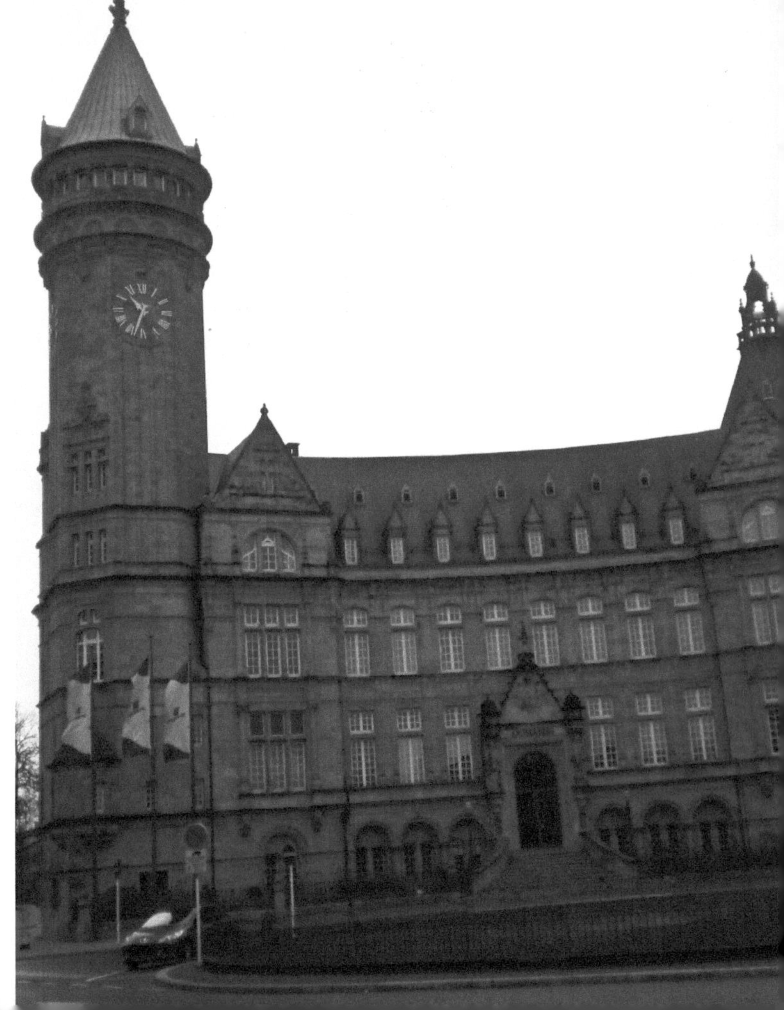

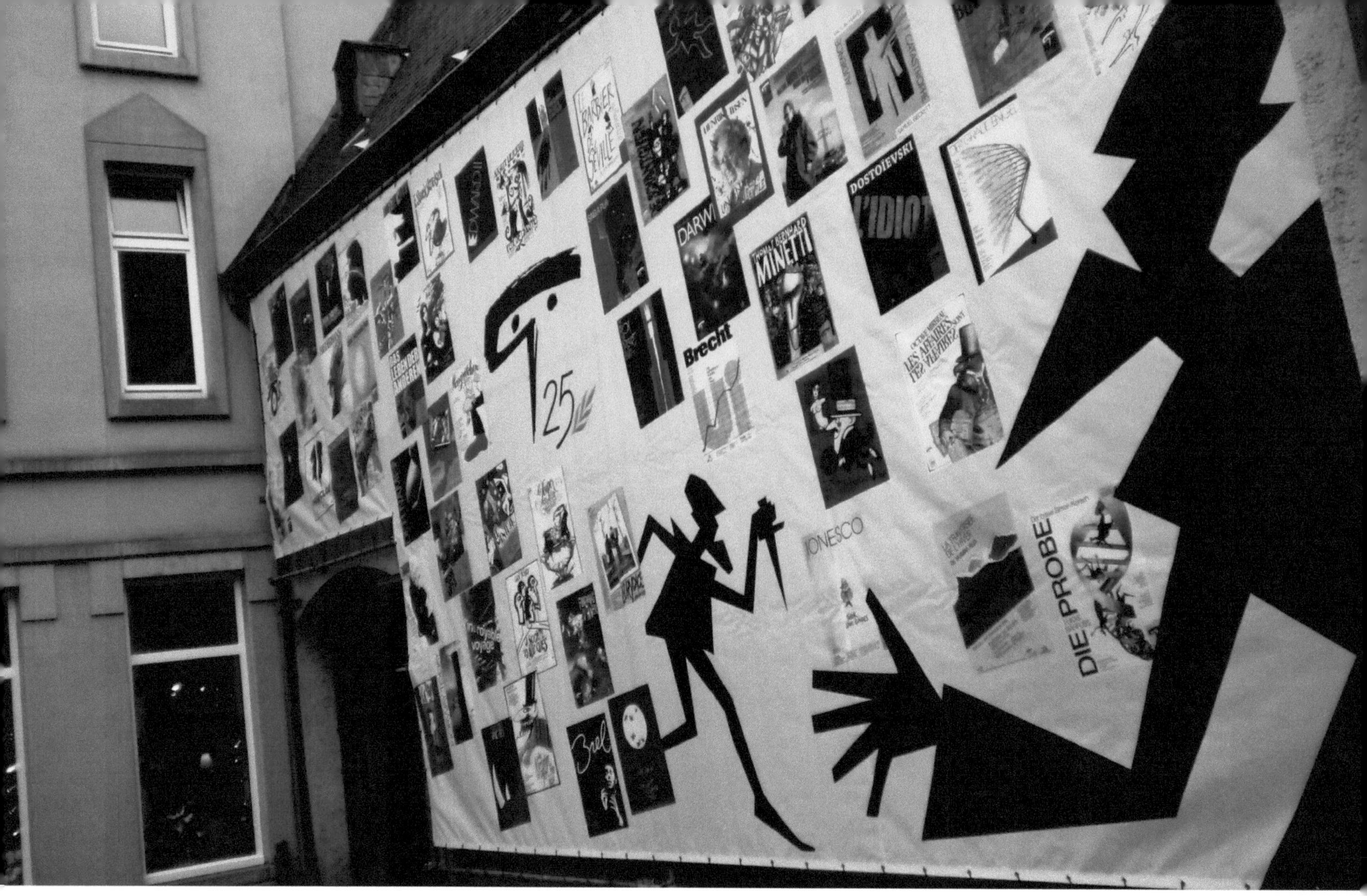

DOSTOIEVSKI
L'IDIOT
DARWI
MINETTI
Brecht
IONESCO
DIE PROBE
25
1985-2010
théâtre des capucins
saison 2009/2010

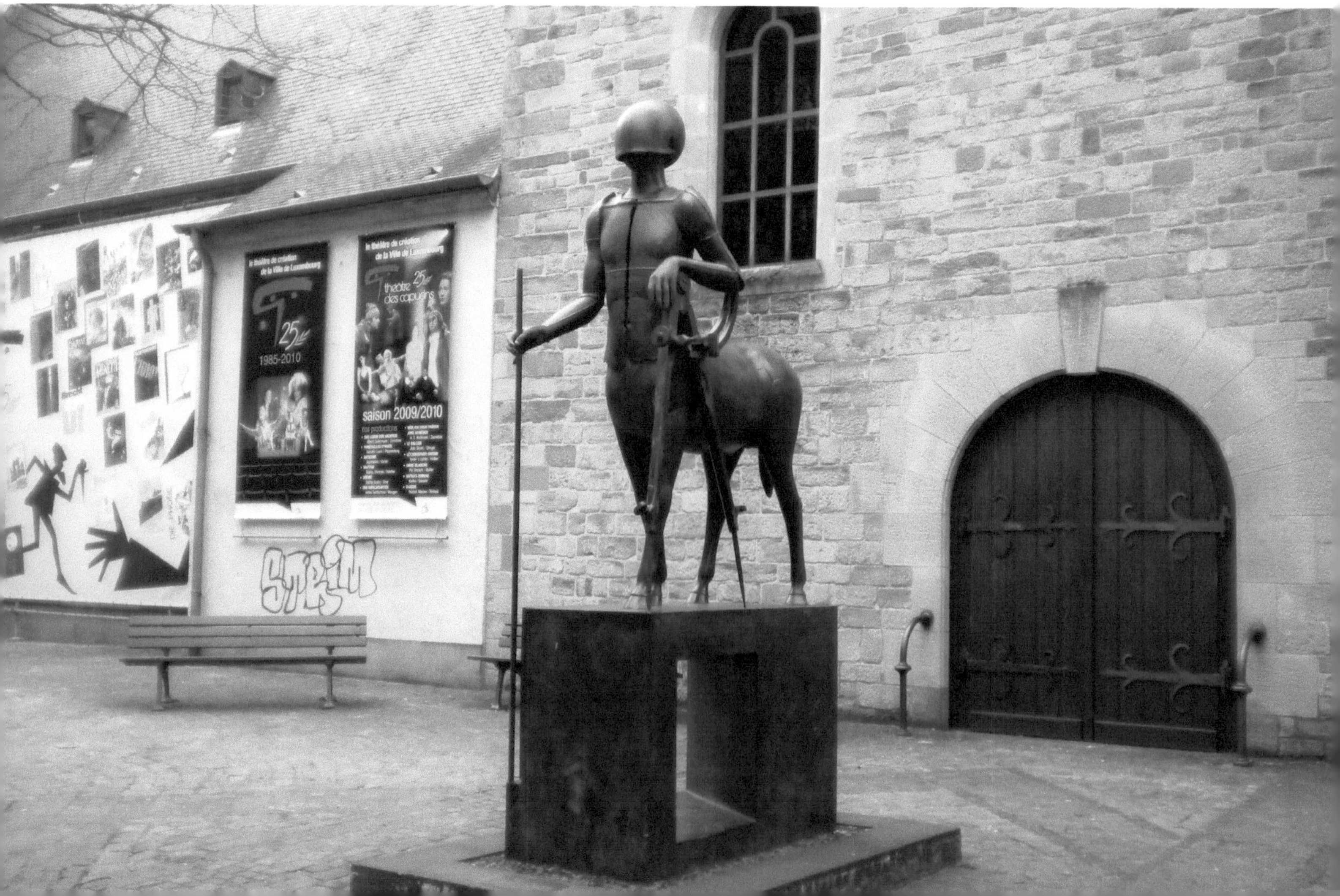

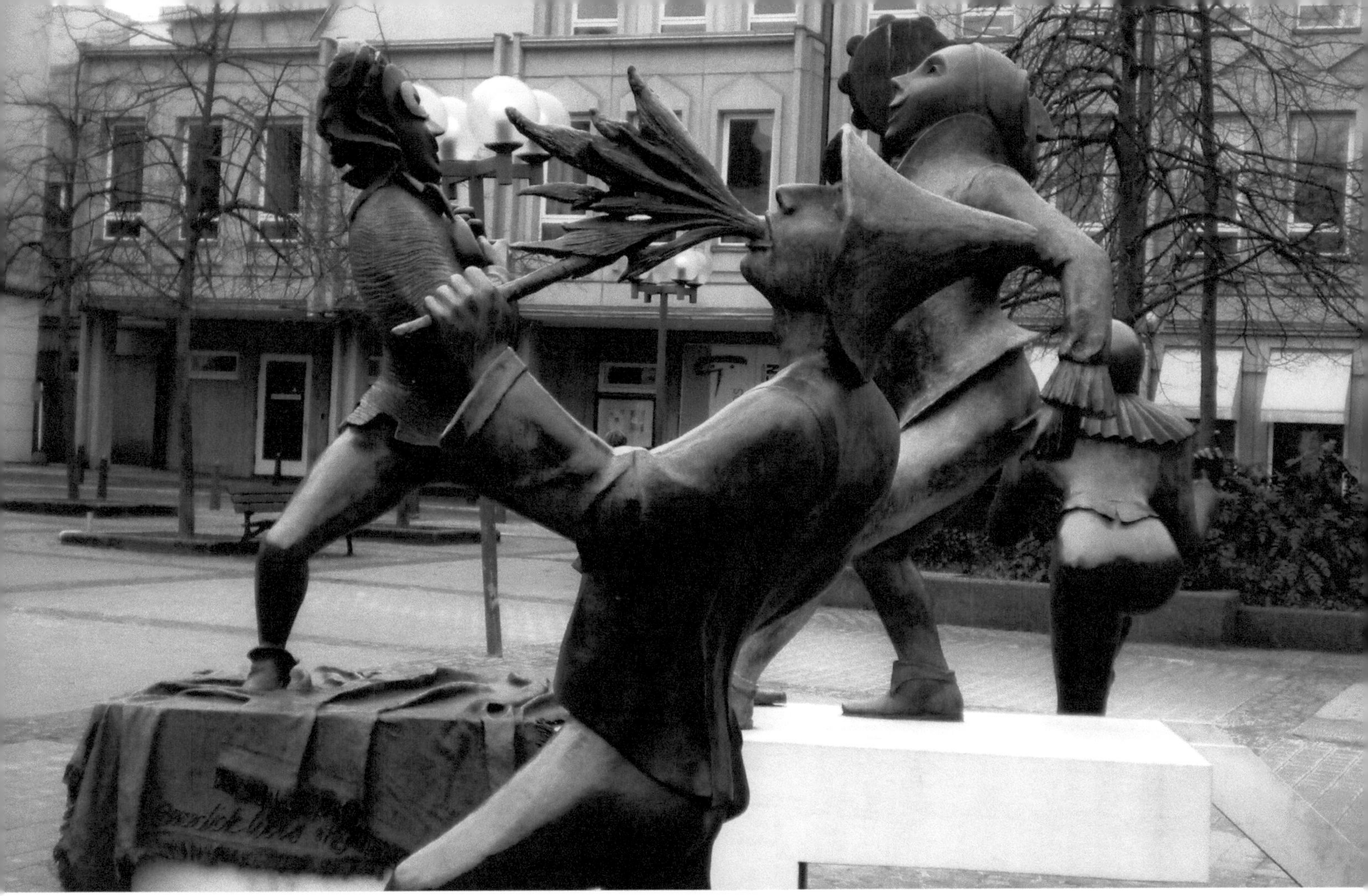

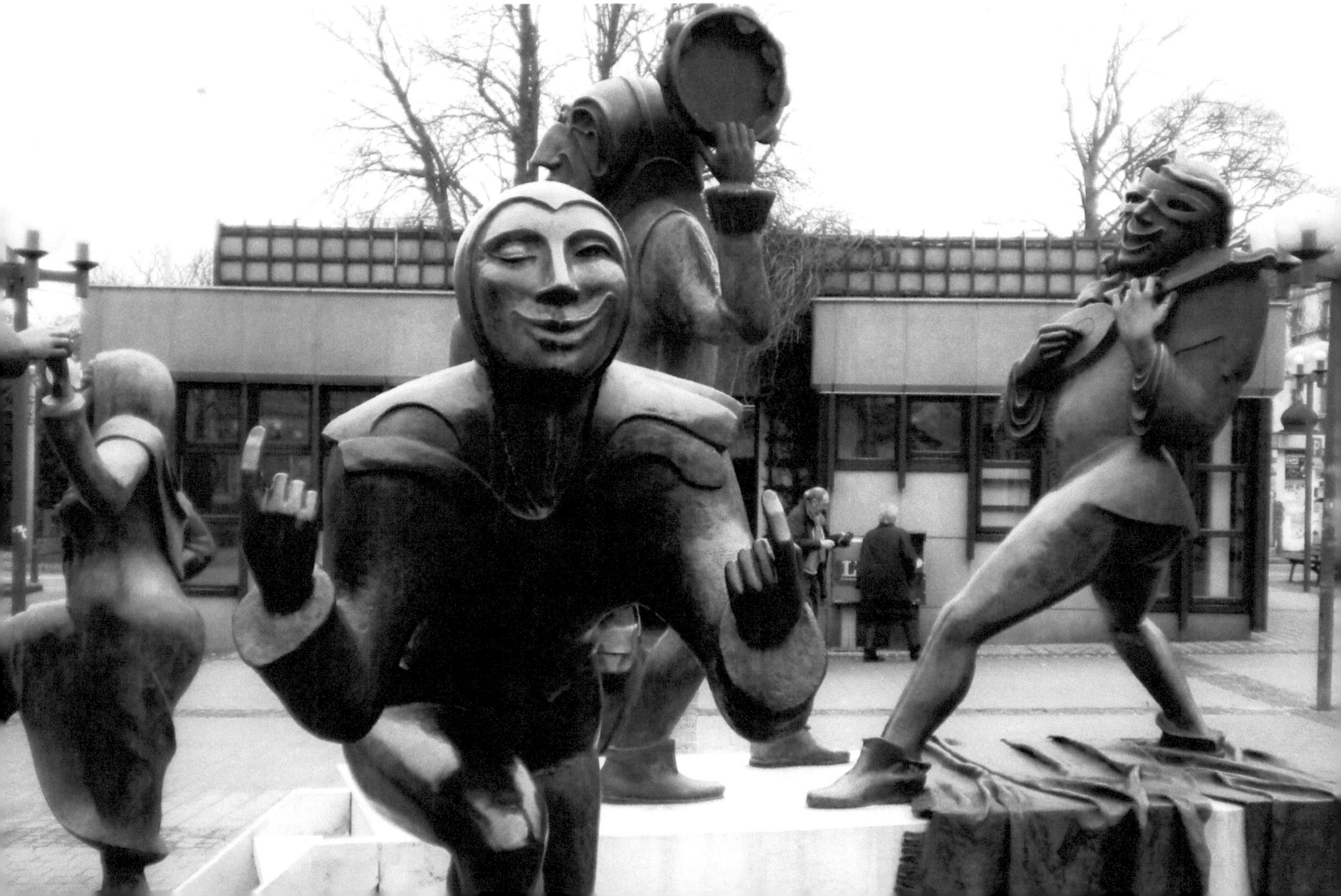

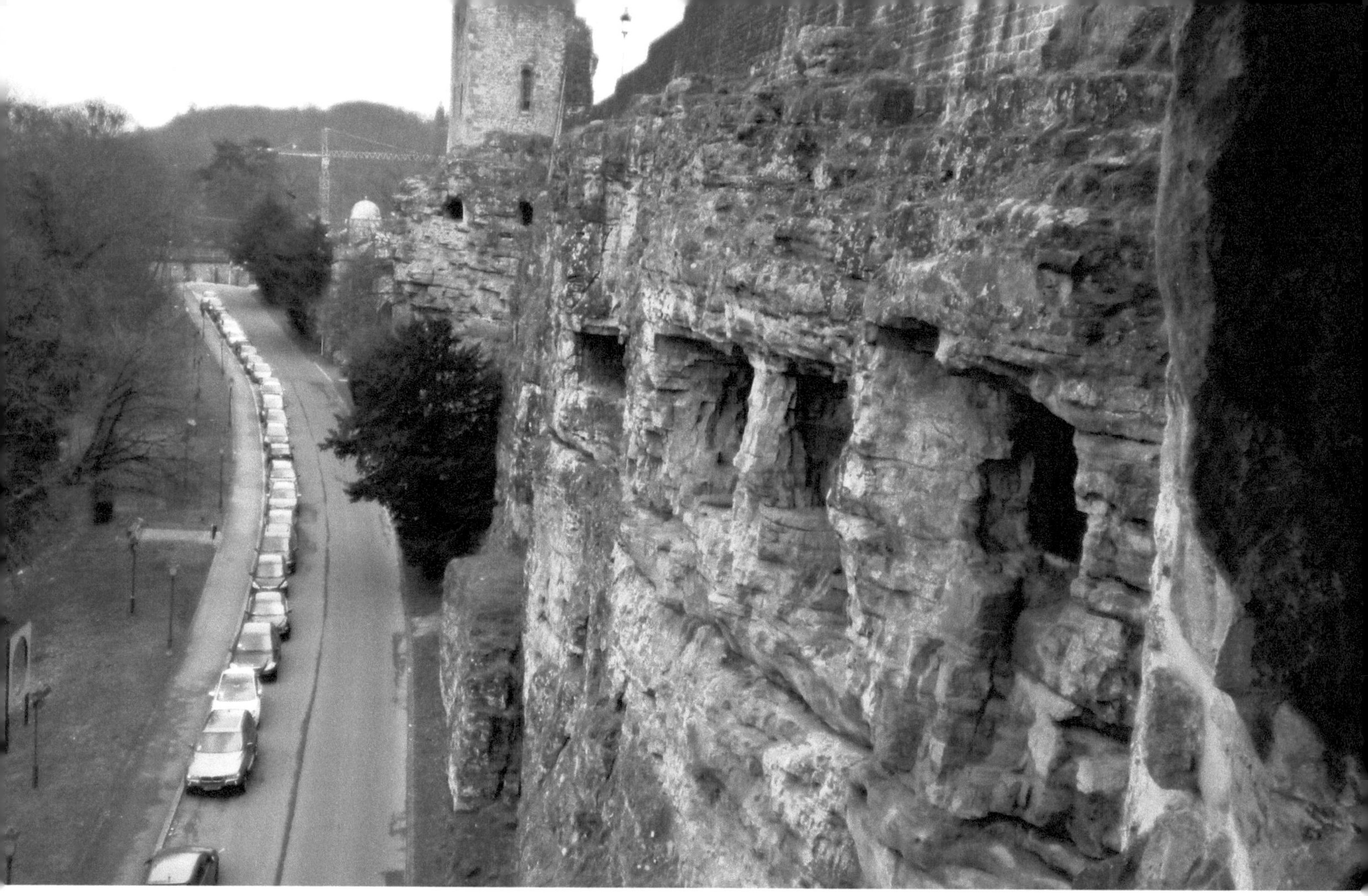

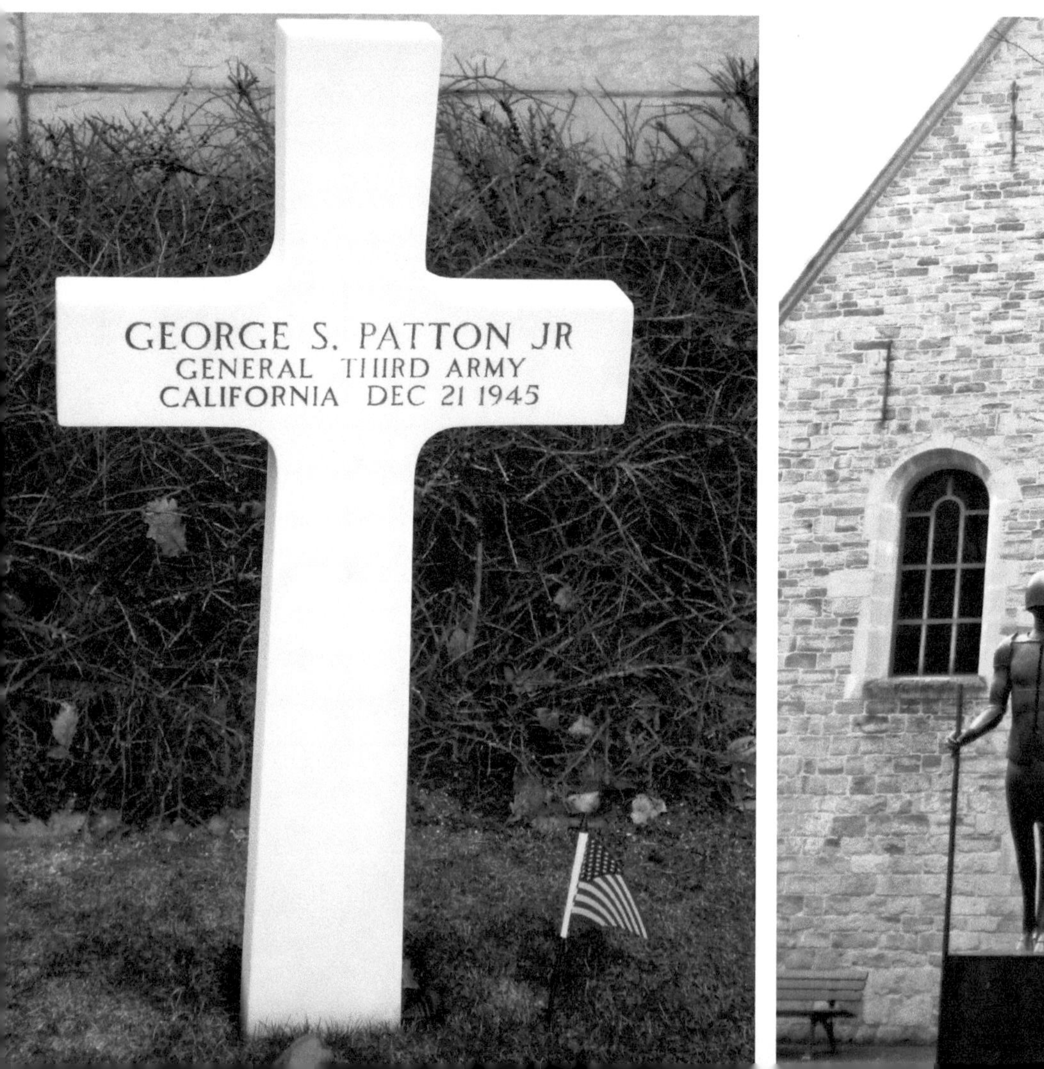
GEORGE S. PATTON JR
GENERAL THIRD ARMY
CALIFORNIA DEC 21 1945

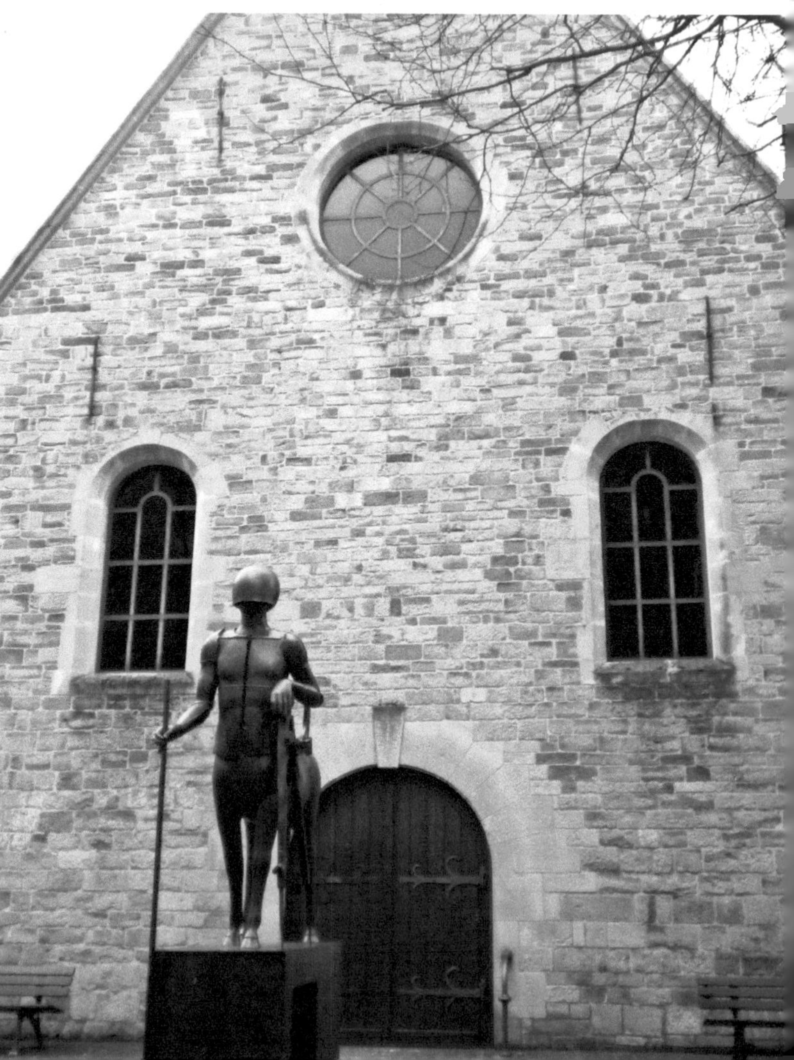

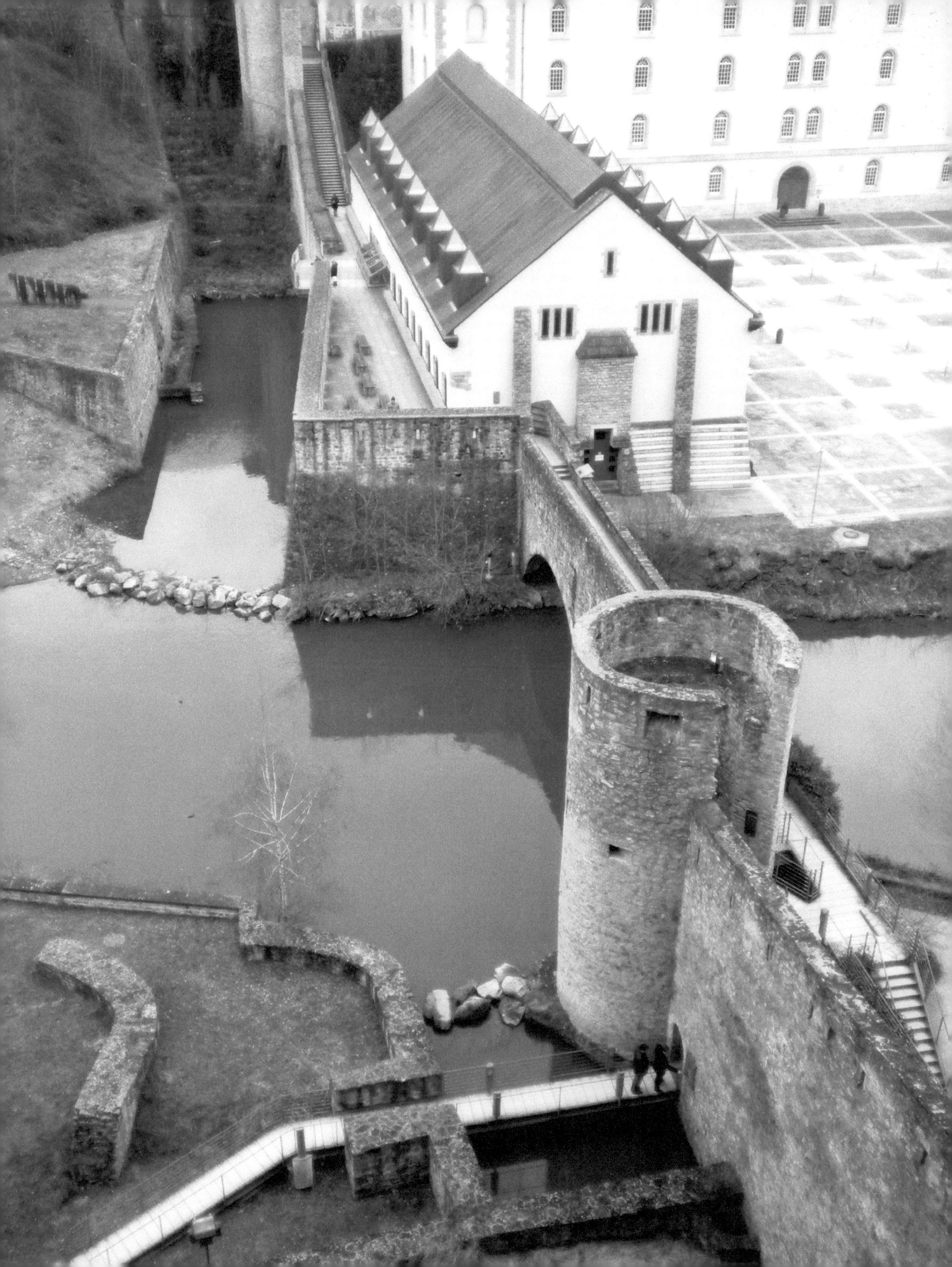

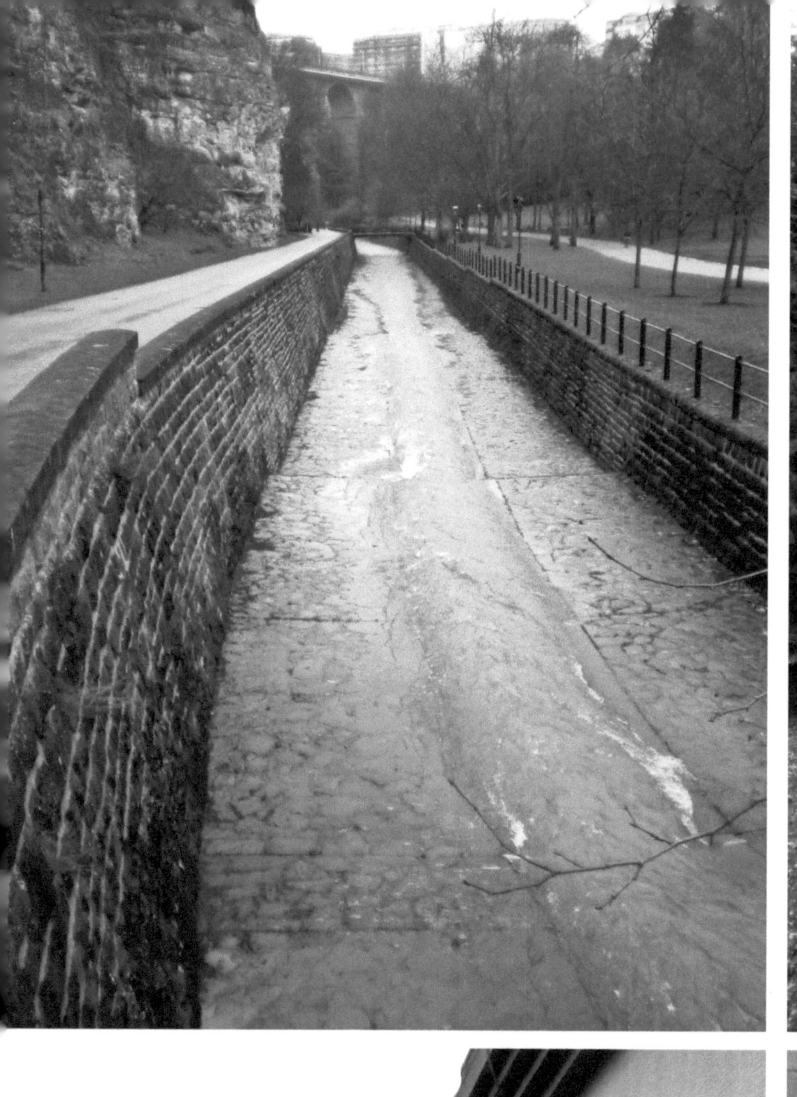

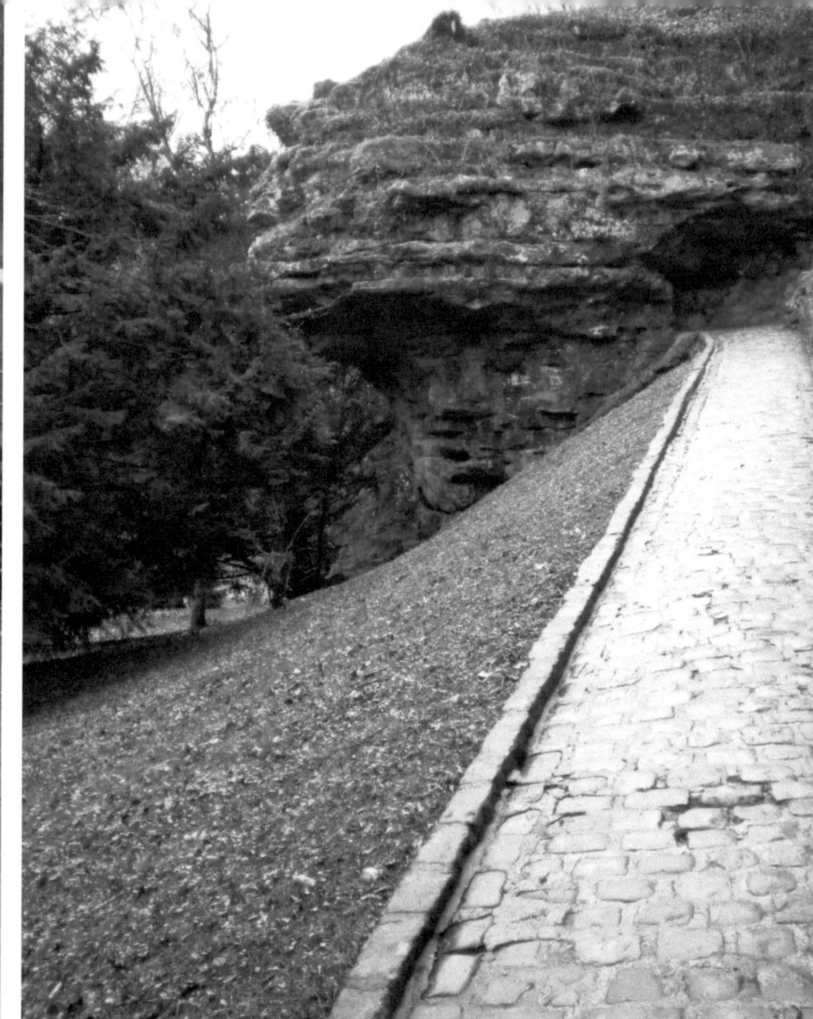

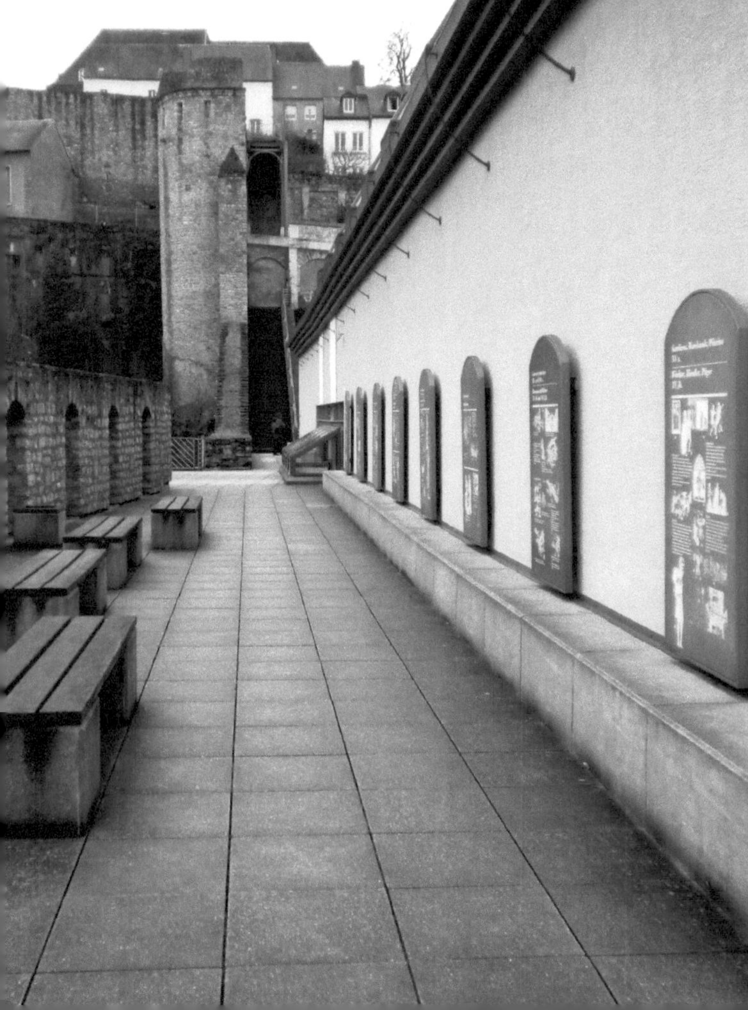

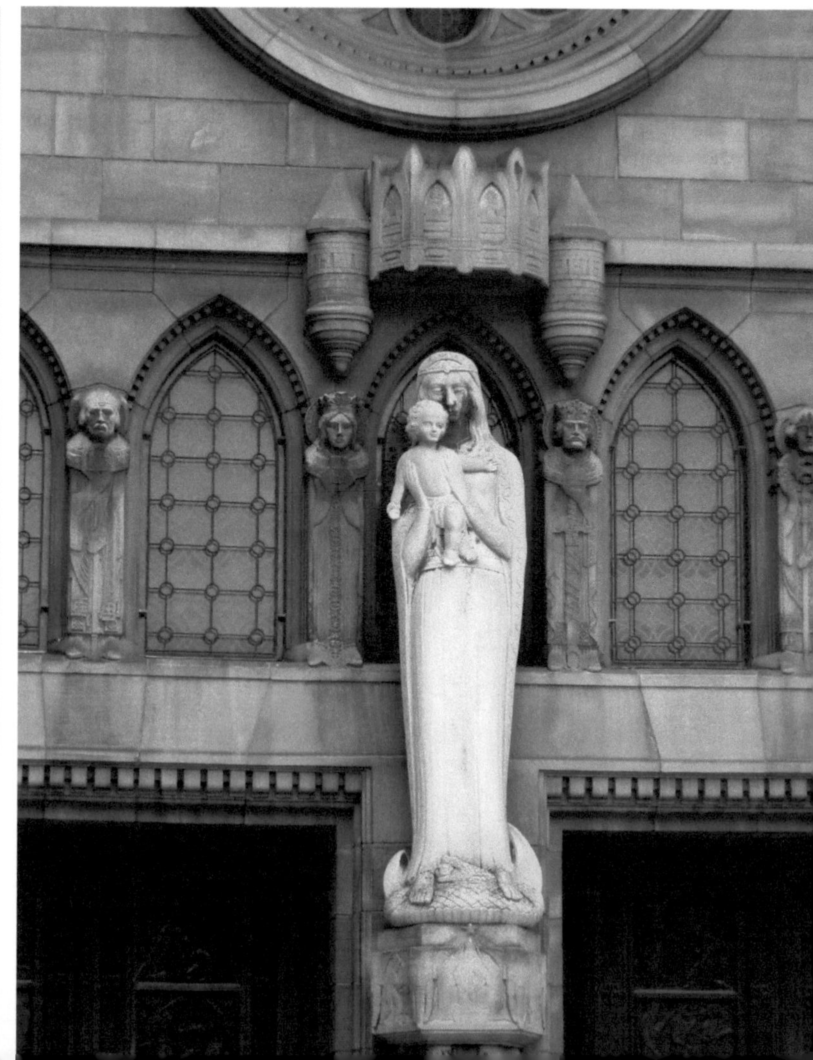

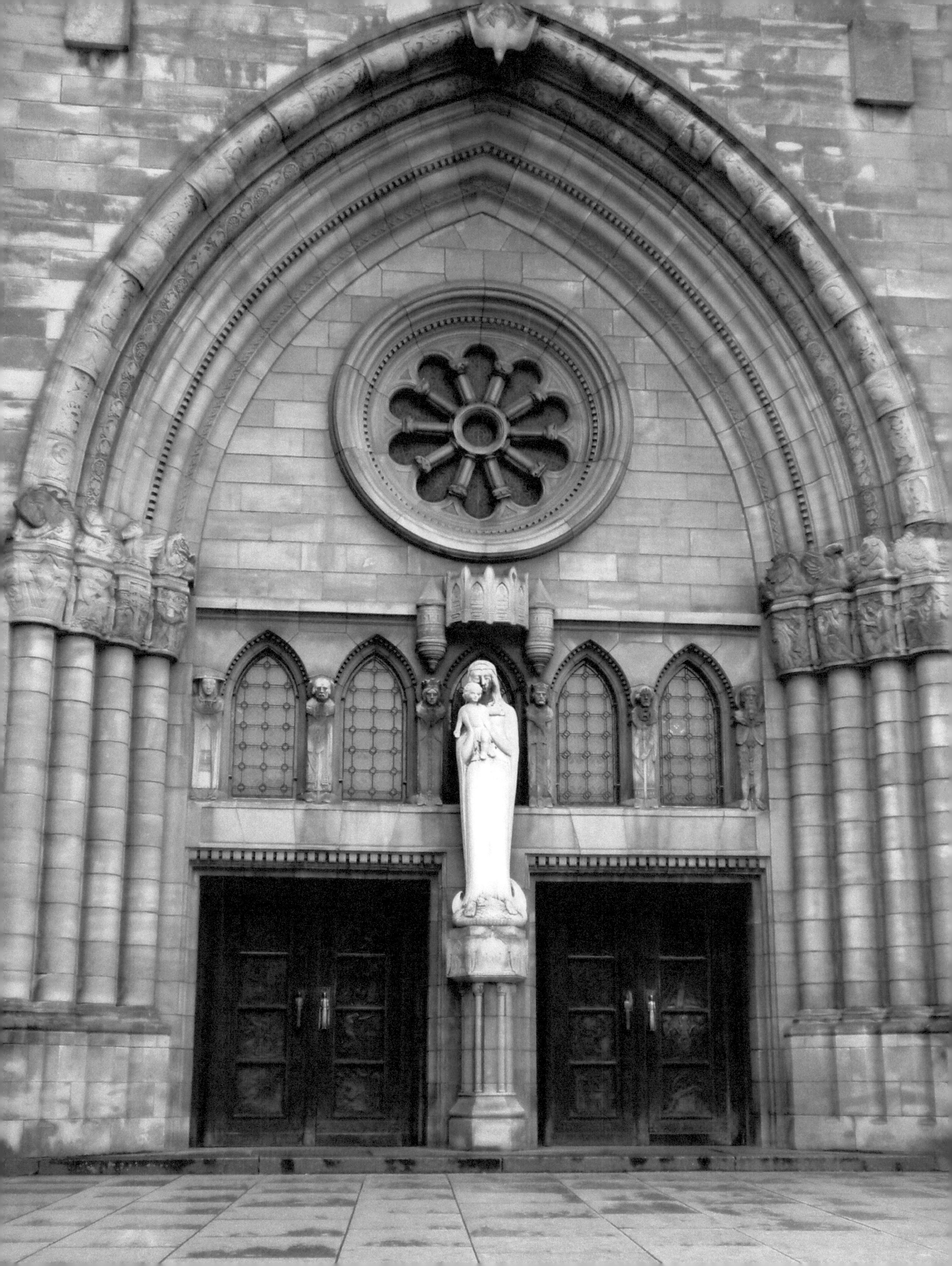

Manama, Bahrain

The following few photos are from Manama, Bahrain. I flew to Bahrain to upgrade some of the network cables that were in the US Embassy. I worked in Bahrain for two months and got to know the country fairly well, Even though I did not do everything I wanted due to the large work load, I enjoyed my time there and would love to visit that country again. If I return to Bahrain, I plan to drive in the Bahrain International Circuit race track. I was sad when I left and was not able to experience the thrill of driving there. I present so few photos from Bahrain due to my poor judgment; I took my film camera and developed the film in Bahrain, a big mistake. Many of my shots are subpar due to poor developing techniques done by the company that developed my film.

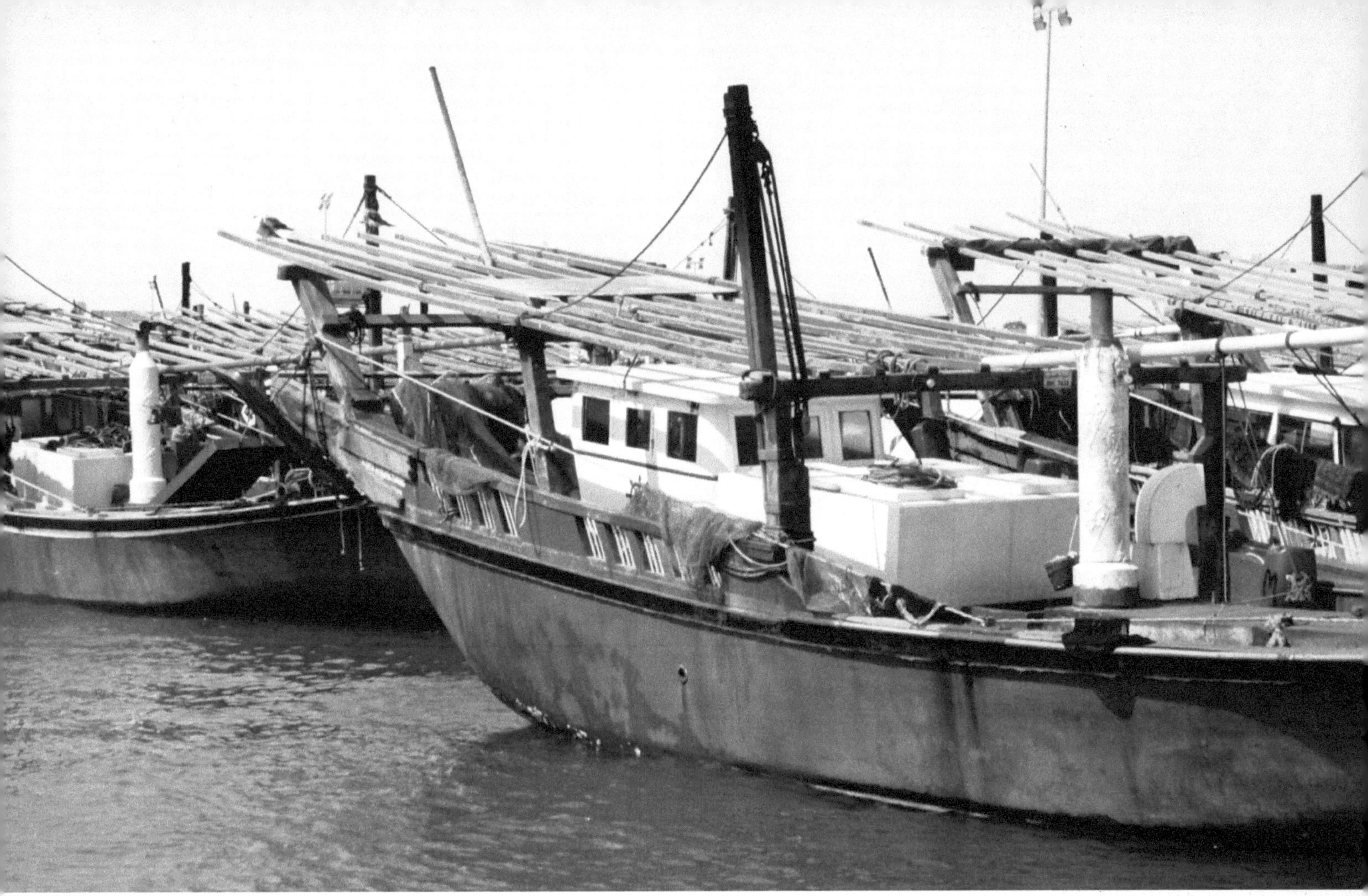

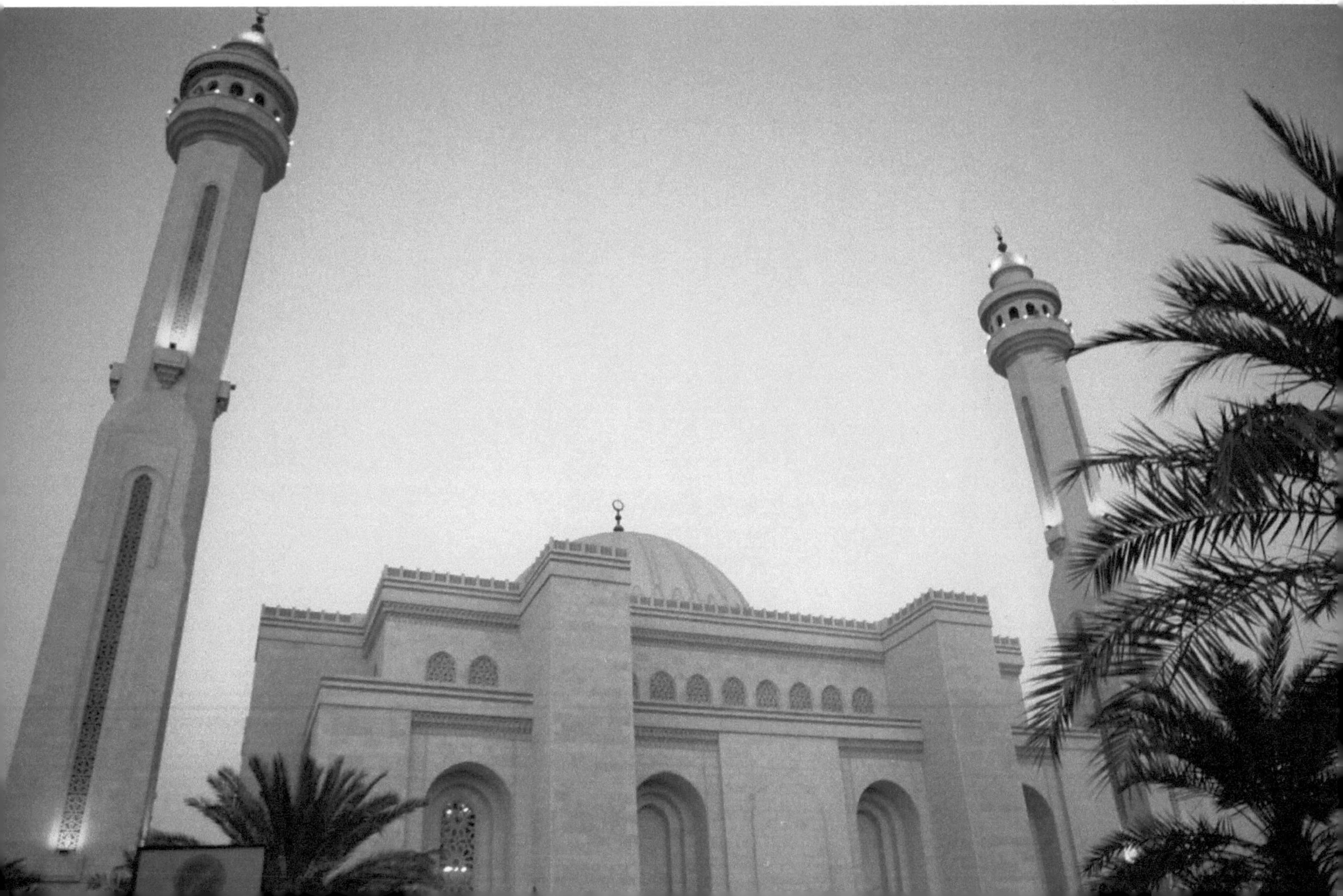

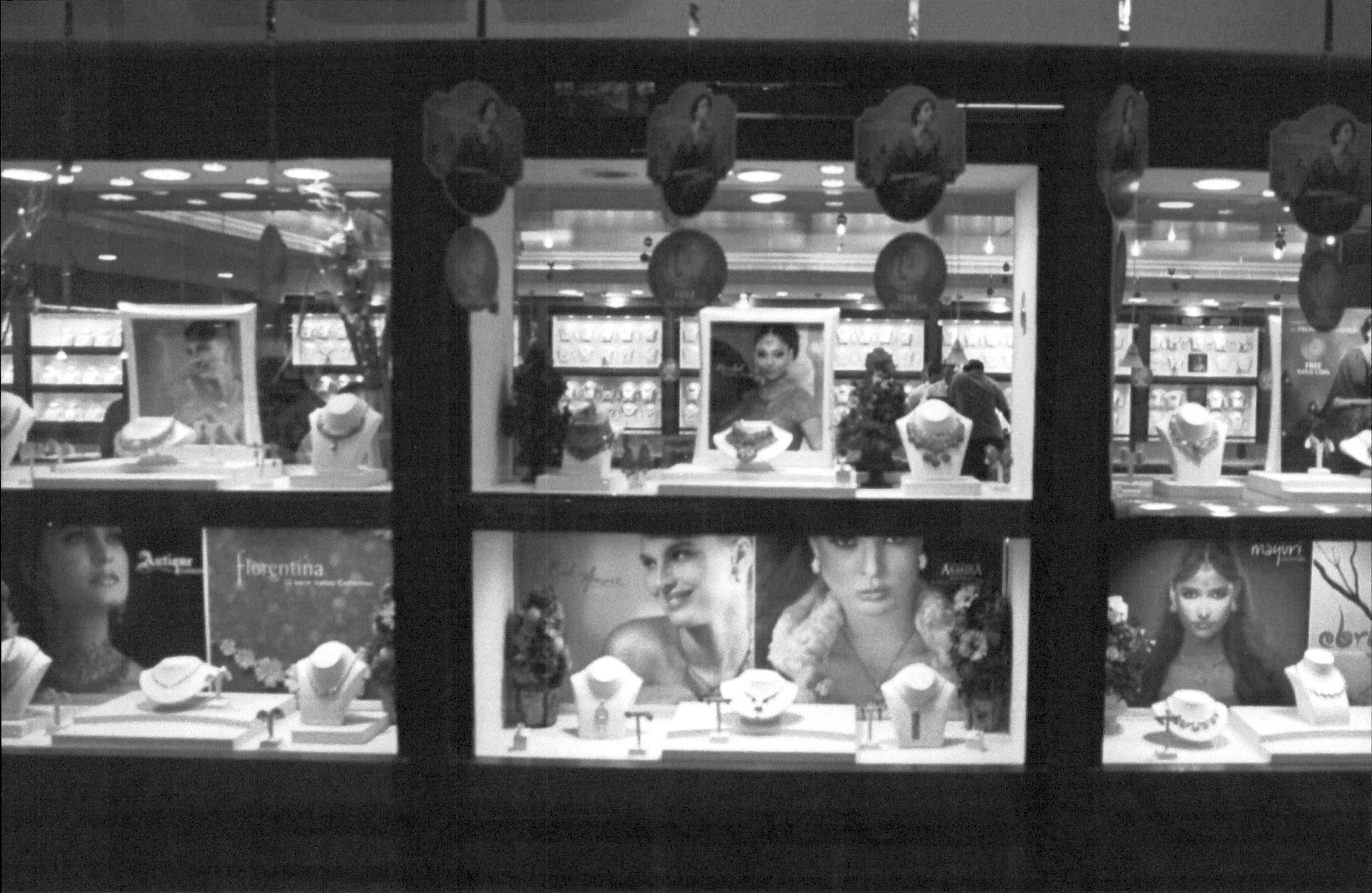

Antique
florentina
mayuri

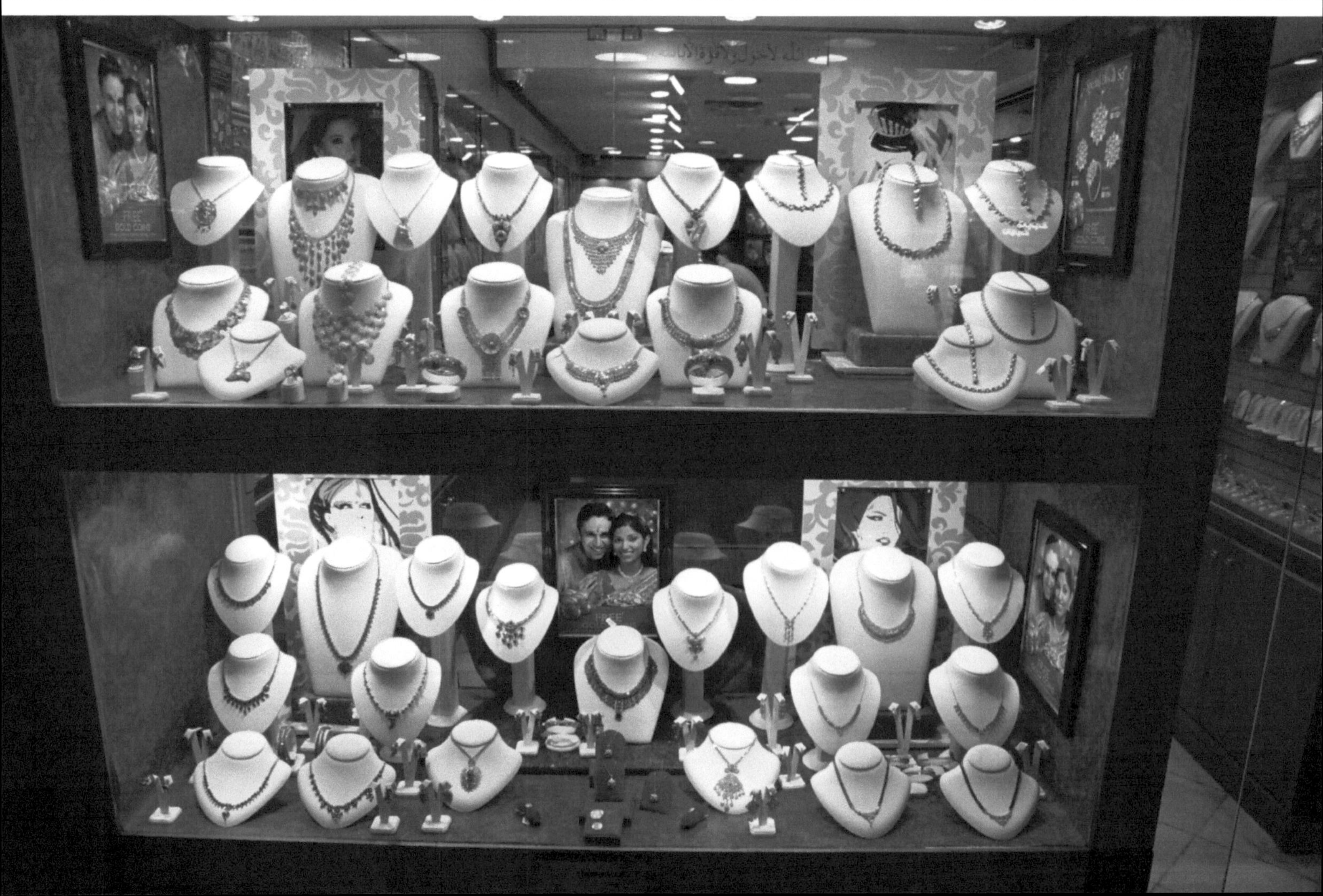

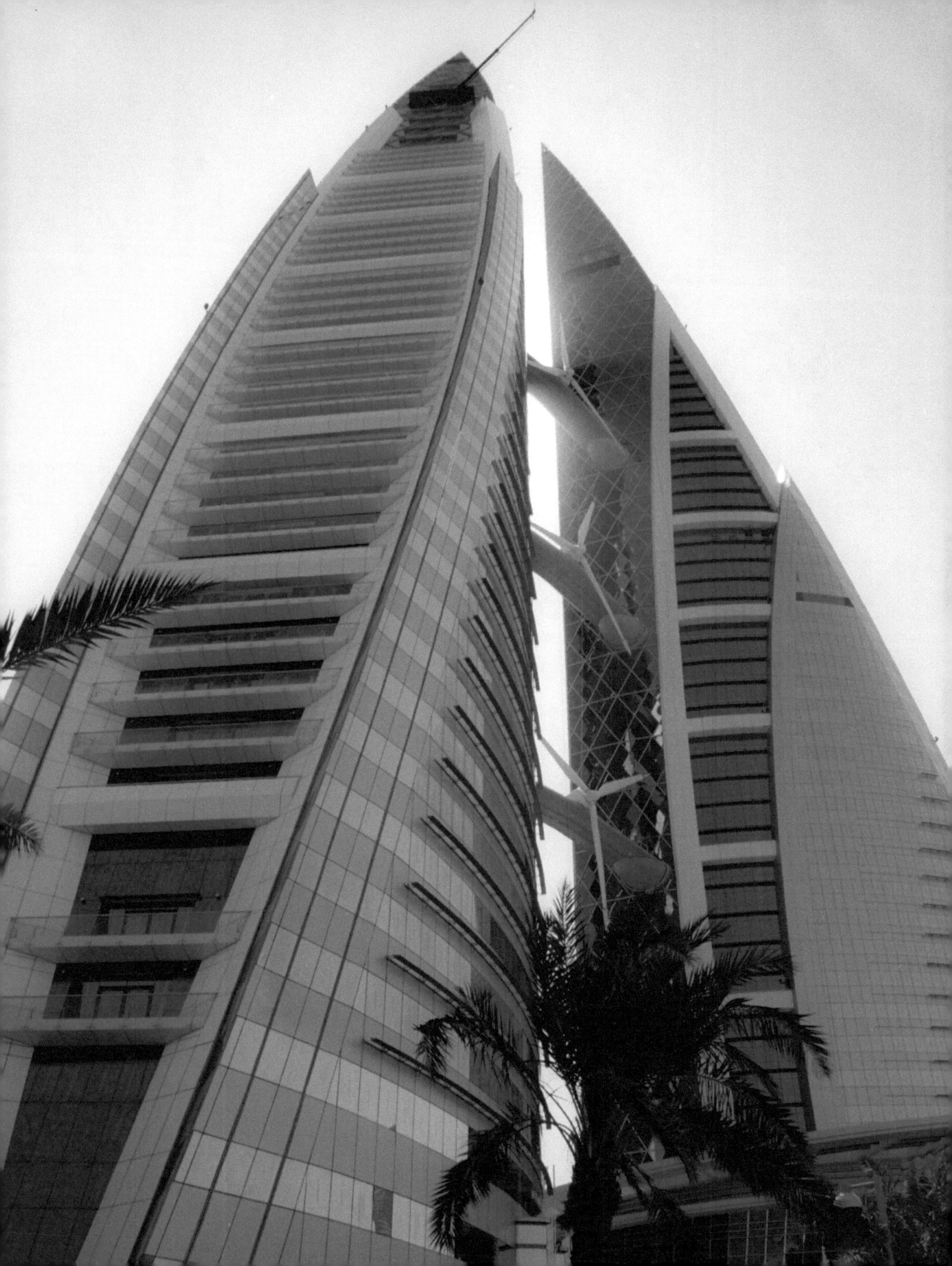

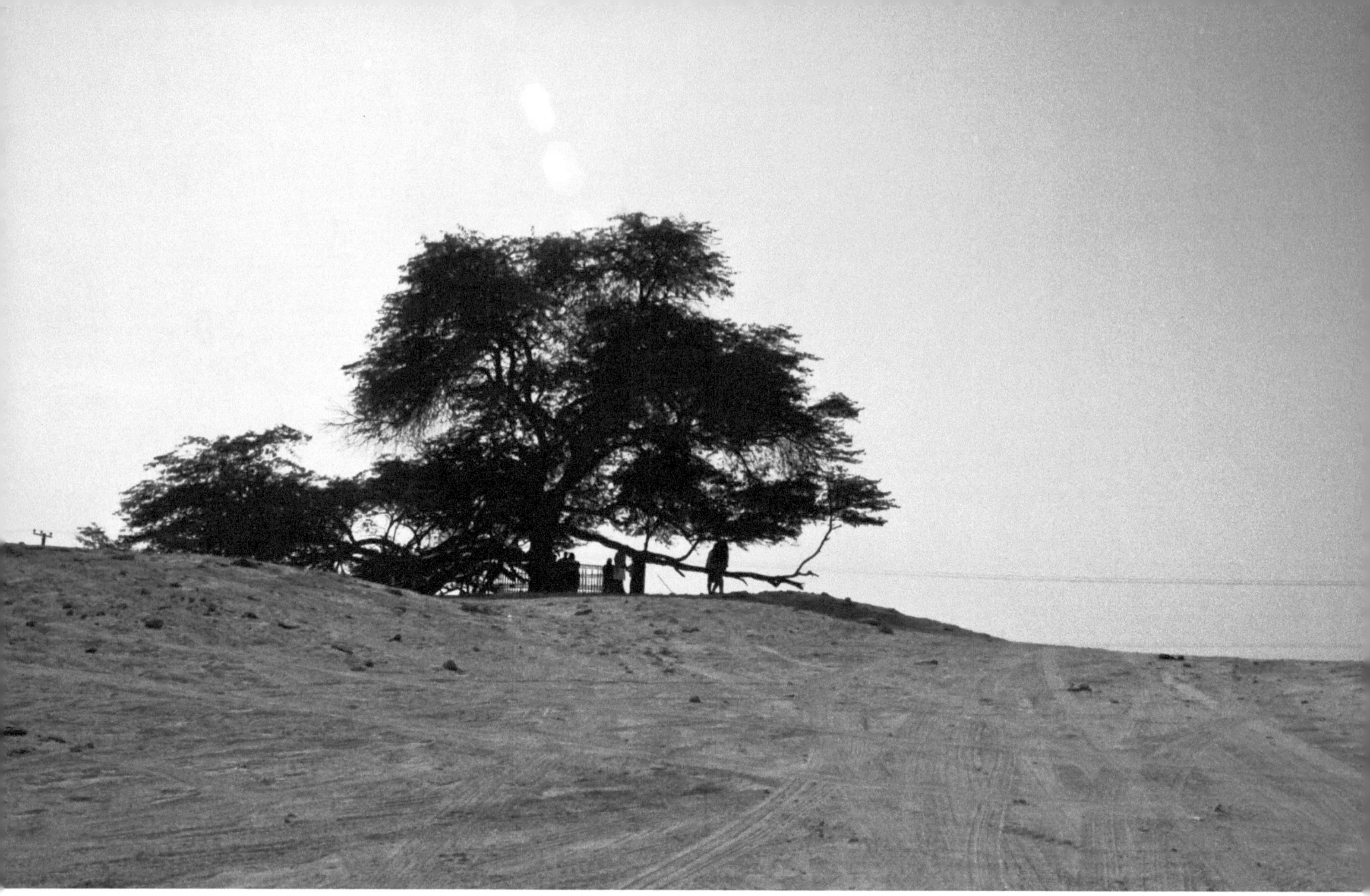

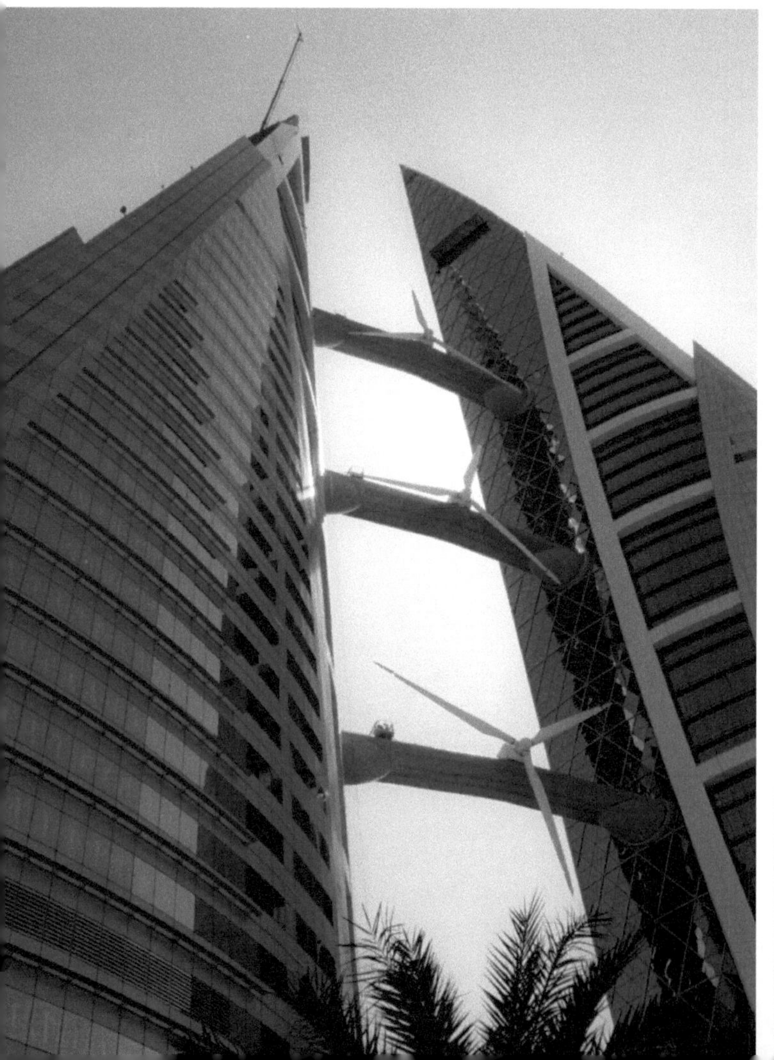

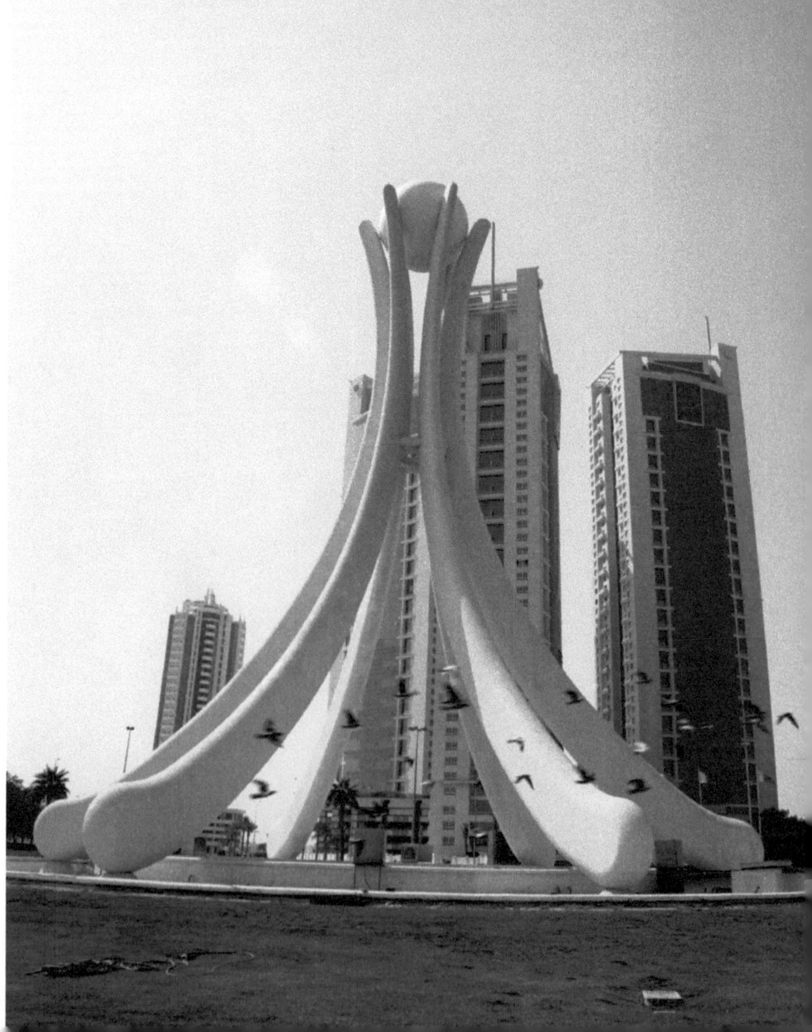

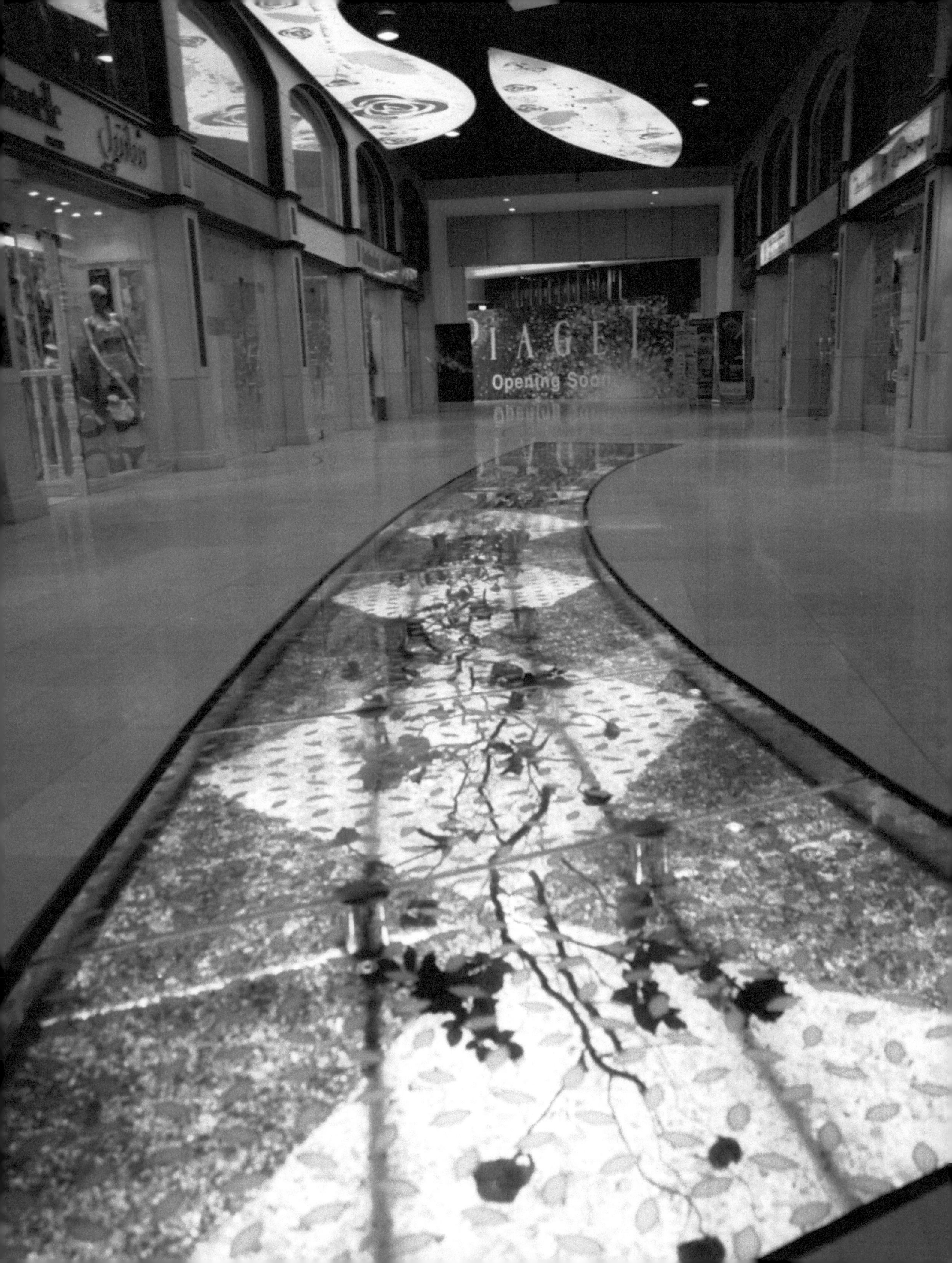
PIAGET
Opening Soon

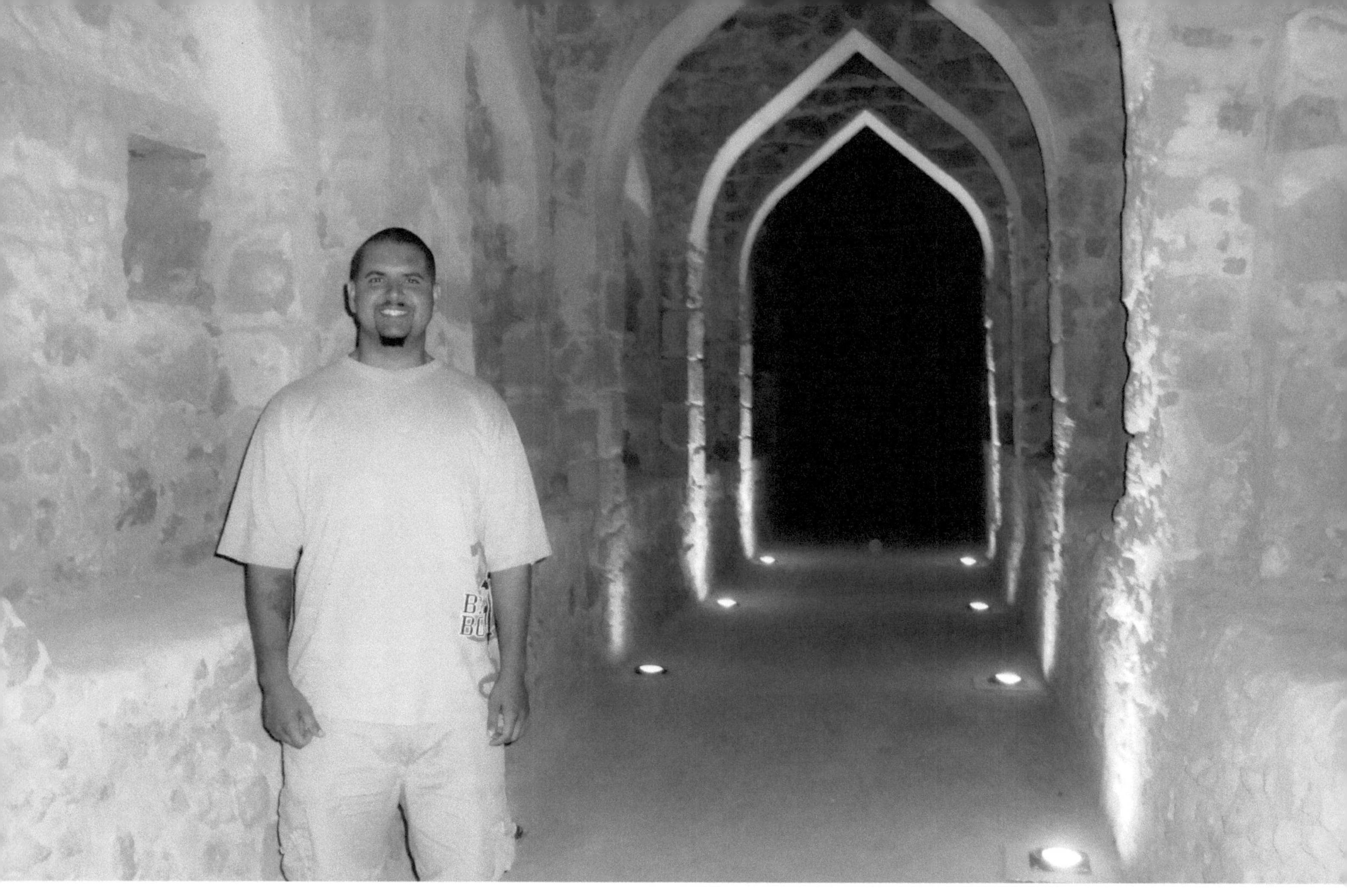

Final Remarks:

I hope you enjoyed the sampling of photos from my various trips. This book has three purposes. The first is to share with you my photos and the beautiful places to which I have traveled. I encourage everyone to visit another country and experience the intricate and subtle beauty this world has to offer at least once in their life. The second purpose is to help raise money for Shriners Hospital, which is a not-for- profit hospital that specializes in treating kids with Orthopedic, Burns, Spinal Cord Injury, Cleft Lip and Cleft Palate. This hospital has treated my eldest daughter for her orthopedic needs. I will be donating 25 percent of profits from this book to Shriners Hospital. If you would like to learn about Shriners Hospital or donate directly, visit www.shrinershq.org/Hospitals/Main. The third purpose of this book is to promote the US Department of State and the wonderful opportunities it gives its employees. Not only do I travel the world, my travels also provide me with a chance to donate my time abroad to those in need. If you are interested in a career with the US Department of State, visit careers.state.gov/officer for more information. If you would like to contact me please email me at foreignservicetraveler@gmail.com. You can also visit my Flickr website to view my current and future projects at www.flickr.com/photos/jamesrivera1.

Special thanks: I want to thank my family for encouraging me and providing me with the inspiration I required. I want to thank Eric Vogel and Joyce Tam for helping me edit my book, their advice helped immensely.

www.ingramcontent.com/pod-product-compliance
Lightning Source LLC
LaVergne TN
LVHW070151110826
845147LV00002B/375

* 9 7 8 0 6 1 5 4 5 3 4 3 9 *